MAKiN' iT

*The Six Universal Habits
for True Survival and
Success*

**By
Edward DeJesus**

This book is dedicated to all youth who have been overlooked and undervalued and to all of the Advocates and Credible Messengers fighting to make sure no youth is overlooked or undervalued again.

And

To my wife, Nicole:
"Happy is the man who finds a true friend, and far happier is he who finds that true friend in his wife." – Franz Schubert

And

To my Grandson,
As you lay nestled in the warmth of my daughter's womb, you have no idea of how much I love you. I dedicate this book to you because Grandpa knows that the greatest danger you will face comes from other people's children. Hurt people hurt people. Healed people heal people. Loved people love people. If I want to make this world safe for you, I must work with other people's children. I did it for your mom, your aunts, and all of your uncles. Now, I do it for you. I love you so much.

This book would not have been possible without the support of a very special team: Nikita Andester, Christian Yonkers, and Devon Boggan. All of your research, editing, and comments are truly appreciated. I also could never have done it without the support of the following individuals who graciously contributed to our crowdfunding campaign. Thank you all for your never-ending support. It means a lot.

Dewayne Upchurch, Farmers Insurance—The Upchurch Agency
Jeff Fleischer, CEO, Youth Advocate Programs
Nora McDowell
Kecia Hawkins
Joseph Bellard
Emile Darquist

Survival Guide Contents

THE INCREDIBLE MESSAGE

I've loved, I've hated, I've cried, I've died inside. I've resurrected, but don't neglect that I've modified

- Logic

What you're holding in your hands is more than just a book: it's a tool to help you succeed. The strategies here were inspired by the stories of authentic young adults who overcame many obstacles to make it. Most of the young people we interviewed didn't finish high school, very few had legal work experience, and almost all had a history in the criminal justice system to some degree. In reflecting on more than thirty years of youth work experience, we've included stories in each chapter about the habits young people needed to develop, the supports they had to acquire, and the skills they mastered before achieving success. To choose six stories from the thousands that have been shared with us over the decades would be like choosing six stars from the midnight sky, taking our focus off the majesty of the Milky Way. We did our best to show you the essence of how to make it. The young people we've worked with these past thirty years kept it real with us—and asked us to give you that same respect.

All the young adults we talked with pointed to several factors impacting success, but they all agreed that a handful stood out above the others—those six Universal Success Habits. They said that if someone is consistently committed to these six habits, they can make it, too, so follow the footsteps of these credible messengers, the young people who have made mistakes and learned before you. If you want to make it, it's your responsibility to work hard at these habits and to connect with others who are also working on these habits.

While writing this book, we came to understand that success is less about the destination and more about the process. Each time you reach a destination, there's another step ahead of you. Each step has its own obstacles, barriers, and setbacks, but if you practice the six habits, you'll meet each and every snag with confidence that the outcome will be in your favor, giving you the courage to plan your next move.

By understanding the delayed-results mindset, you'll learn how to formulate better strategies, objectives, supports, and resources, combining them into a solid action plan to get you through to your next destination. After a while, obstacles won't seem much like hurdles at all. You'll have become an expert, able to apply your unique awareness and the collective wisdom of those who preceded you to breeze through the barriers that would have once held you back.

We won't lie, getting into MAKiN iT shape takes plenty of work—this journey's not a one-and-done deal. But by consistently moving towards success, you can hone the internal strength you need to get there. You don't get strong from just one pushup, and like hitting the gym, MAKiN iT only gives you results thanks to your continued effort and dedication to your end goal. To help you along the way, we've included plenty of exercises, but it's up to you to do them. MAKiN iT isn't something that happens to you; it's something you make happen.

Let's get to work.

1

Hold your head up, there's a light in the sky. I know your fed up but you must try to survive. Each moment's precious, don't let life pass you by. Keep focused, keep your eyes on the prize.

- Macklemore

UNIVERSAL SUCCESS HABIT ONE:

Successful Young People Consistently Make Moves to Advance their Lives, Freedom, and Future Economic Opportunity.

The bus window was cool against Angel's temple. He sighed and raised his eyebrows, watching the street whir past him. How'd he wind up here? Struggling like always. He'd dropped out the month before after flunking tenth grade. Again. Who was he fooling in trying? No diploma, not enrolled in a GED class, and no job prospects in sight. At seventeen, with nothing to show for himself other than a pocket of change and friends he smoked with, getting hired was hard. Something had to give. That afternoon, just like basically every day before, his friends asked him to smoke in the park. Angel checked his clock on his phone: 4:40 – there was still time to do something else.

"Nah, man. I already made plans with someone right now. I'm late."

It wasn't a lie; he just didn't tell them that they weren't exactly plans he'd made — or that he was going to the library. It had all started the day before. Angel was chilling at Starbucks, waiting for his shorty to get off from work. A man with Angel's complexion and build was sipping on a latte next to him, reading. His outfit was sharp: a tailored suit with a pair of clean Air Jordan 11 Retros and a blue silk skinny tie, a nice contrast to his salt and pepper hair. The man's head hung low, buried deep in a book. Angel craned his neck, pretending to stretch left and right, to catch the book title. The man raised his eyebrows, tilting the book so he could see the title, a smile tugging at the corners of his mouth. Busted! Angel looked away, back towards the counter—but not before he saw the name along the book's spine.

"Hey, lil' bro," the man said. "You like to read?"

"Not really man, I'm not too much into that."

The man leaned back. "It's the way up and out."

Angel shook his head. "I don't know, man. Seems like one hell of a way to waste a day."

The man smiled at Angel before returning to his book. "If you say so."

For the next fifteen minutes, Angel tried – and failed – to peep the title. The man stretched and stood, tucking the book into his bag. Before heading out the door, he rested his fingertips on Angel's table.

"Name's Ed." He stuck out his hand.

Brow's raised, Angel slowly shook Ed's hand and gave his name.

"I wrote a book – just came out. Who knows? Could be the one that convinces you to start reading. Tomorrow I'm reading some of it in a showcase – you should come. It's 4:30 at the main library downtown."

Angel took in this man's confidence and fresh clothes. He didn't seem as dried up as other adults who'd offered him advice – maybe this guy would have at least something worthwhile to say. "Yeah – I don't know. Maybe."

"Think about it, man." And with that, Ed was gone.

Angel sighed on the bus now, thinking about Ed's sharp outfit and his library book. Angel didn't know what he hoped to find at the reading – and was so late he didn't even know if he'd make it. But hey, if that guy had been so fly and reading a book, maybe the library was just as good a starting point as any for breaking his depressing routine. What did the library even look like these days? He struggled to remember the last time he'd gone in one – would he even know how to find Ed's reading?

He'd been so lost in his looping thoughts that Angel hadn't realized the bus had stopped until the driver stood up and shouted, "We're having some engine trouble – everybody off!" before lumbering down the steps and stretching his back in the waning afternoon sun.

Angel checked his phone, the cracks in his screen spider-webbing *over the time: 5:15. Great. The library closed in forty-five minutes. He hopped off the bus and walked briskly toward the library, eager to shave off some minutes. His feet ached, the soles of his shoes long worn flat. The man reading had been wearing such fresh shoes. How did he manage to get there, buying a new pair without scraping together quarters and dollar bills? Angel couldn't even imagine the kind of job he'd need to get there. When he'd been in school, he'd always enjoyed the visual things—art, geometry, computer lab. When he'd been in school. But he'd dropped out, had nothing. Angel shook his head, trying to rattle loose the endless negative thoughts going through his dome, and so as he picked up his pace, whirring past shops with young people flowing in and out, passing a coffee shop where everyone was working on computers or bonding over steaming mugs. When Angel had been eleven, his aunt (estranged from him since a falling out with his mom) had taken him to a coffee shop like that. Angel had been so fascinated by the aroma and the screaming of the milk steamer; his aunt had talked him through the list of lattes and cappuccinos, helping him pick the right one out. He'd settled on a dirty chai, and the spice had tickled his tongue and bubbled up to his nose; he'd loved it. His aunt was a graphic designer. Had been, anyway. He had no idea what she was up to now. Angel felt bitter relief that she had no idea what he'd become. Let her remember him as a hopeful little boy with two small hands hugging a white mug. Angel sighed.*

By 5:40, he reached the library doors and pulled them open, cool air churning onto his face. "We close in twenty minutes!" The woman at the desk was stacking books onto a cart.

"I know. Is that presentation happening still?"

"No, it finished about fifteen minutes ago." Seeing Angel's shoulders sag, her face softened. "Go upstairs to the community room – maybe the speaker is still there packing up and you can see what it was all about."

Angel raced up the steps, following signs for the community room. By the time he came to the door, he was out of breath – and all the lights were off. He was too late. Swearing under his breath, Angel turned around to head home. He was stupid for even trying. That guy probably didn't even really expect him to show up. At the landing in the middle of the stairs, a painting caught his eye, looming and ominous. The devil was smiling over a chess board, across from a young man clutching his baseball cap, perplexed. On a gold plate above the painting the title was engraved: "Checkmate?"

CHECKMATE?

www.edwarddejesus.com

Angel's throat tightened up. Why would they put this painting up right here? The title was mocking him – he didn't have another move. This was it. He'd backed himself into a corner. No diploma, no GED, and he could hardly afford the bus fare. Who was he kidding? Nothing in Ed's book could have helped him anyway. Angel closed his eyes and leaned against the wall beside the painting, sliding to the floor and tilting his chin up, humiliated by the tears gathering in the corners of his eyes.

He didn't hear the soft tread of boots brushing against the carpeted stairs until they reached the landing. Opening his eyes, Angel saw a security guard standing over him.

"Yeah, yeah, man. You're closing. I know. I need a second, though."

"Son, you okay?" Angel opened his eyes again, his brows knitted together. Had he just asked if Angel was okay?

The guard held his hand out, down towards Angel on the floor. "Name's Jim."

Angel took his hand and shook it. "Angel. And I'm okay. It's just...this painting got me. It's hard, realizing there's no way out."

Jim smiled. "The title there would say different."

"Huh?"

"The title of the painting. 'Checkmate?' It's a question, not a statement. Look, I spent ten years behind bars. When I was there, I had a lot of time to think my life over." He settled against the wall beside Angel. "A lot. And the first few months, I got close with the same type of crowd I'd been with on the outside—people who had landed me there in the first place. But one day, I was fed up." He glanced at Angel. "Wanna know what I did?"

5

Angel's eyes had been pinned to Jim since he'd said he'd been in prison. "What?"

"I took up chess." He chuckled. "I'm serious. I did nothing but play, making friends with the chess players instead. Sometimes I'd even play against myself, and once I got out, I got into local and regional competitions—it was around the same time I started working here. I still do them. And when they brought this painting in, it filled me with a lot of hope."

"How, man?"

"The title's telling it like it is – the young man up there, he's got another move!" He motioned toward the painting with one arm. "The game isn't over for him. Just look at the board. Anybody who plays chess can see it. It isn't check, and it damn sure ain't checkmate. It's not over for that kid just yet." He clapped Angel on the shoulder and stood up, his knees popping. "And it's not over for you, either." Looking Angel over, he held out his hand to help him up. "Now what was it you were looking for?"

Angel hesitated, then accepted Jim's hand and hoisted himself up. "I was trying to make it to this talk. I, that guy, Ed," he gestured upstairs in the direction of the community room. "He told me I should come. I almost didn't. I guess I was just hoping he'd be able to point me in the right direction." Angel looked away. "It was stupid."

"You the kid he met at Starbucks?"

"What?" Angel cocked his head at Jim. "Yeah, man."

Jim smiled. "Well, before Ed left, he handed me a book and said he'd hoped to give it to a kid he'd met at Starbucks the day before. I'm guessing that's you. Here." Jim pulled a slim paperback out of his inner coat pocket and handed it to Angel. The book's title: MAKiN' iT. Ed was smiling on the inner flap, and a piece of paper flitted from between the pages and to the floor – it was a note:

> Lil' bro,
>
> Call me if you need help – with anything.

His number was at the bottom.

Jim peered over his shoulder. "Looks like you got yourself another move."

Angel had another move—and so do you. Despite past involvement with

1.1. The Jump-Off

the criminal justice system and drugs, despite problems with school, thousands upon thousands of young adults like yourself manage to make it each year. They graduate from high school or earn that GED. They find and keep jobs, attend college, raise families, and give back to their communities. You may have taken a few wrong steps along the way, yet you remain—and always will be—more than just the sum of your mistakes. Everyone develops at a different pace, and you shouldn't be judged by anyone (including yourself) for your own timeline.

If you're reading this, then it's likely that an adult labeled you "at-risk at some point." What they didn't realize is that you're not at-risk—you're "at-opportunity." Even right now, by cracking open this book, you've proved that you have what it takes to make it, and you possess more resilience than most people can understand. Why? Because you moved past all the obstacles mounted against you to get here. And you made it. Congratulations—you're at the starting line for your success.

You probably weren't born with a silver spoon in your mouth, but don't go thinking you're emptyhanded. You're rich in a long history of others who overcame a lot to become something great. And if all those people could do it, then you can too.

Most older folks try to pretend that their generation never had any issues, that they blossomed right into adulthood as saints. The truth is that each generation has had beef with the generations that came before them. The weed-smoking hippies of the sixties grew into the Wall Street execs of the eighties, leading this country to its greatest economic recession in eighty years. Those dropouts of the seventies are now the ones regulating the information superhighway. And the party animals of the eighties? They're now raking it in as the Shark Tank entrepreneurs of today. It's high time that you and your generation get yours.

What trapped the young people of earlier generations and may be tripping you up now is a survival mindset. When you're in survival mode and caught in an immediate-results environment, the wants of today become stronger than the glimmering promise of tomorrow. You develop immediate-results habits, reinforced by a society that glorifies the fast, the now, and the moment. The problem is that the first prerequisite for success is shifting that mindset to a delayed-results one. Unfortunately for us, hundreds of thousands of years of evolution pushes us back into that "gimmee now" mentality.

We develop habits through the continuous use of tools, beliefs, values, and behaviors. If you think about it, people wake up in the morning holding onto the same attitudes about school that they had all year. They hold the same old beliefs about opportunity, never really getting out there or never really trying to get a job. They let their disappointments or fear of failure be their reason for giving up. Maybe they're saying they value education, yet they can't remember the last time they put in more than two hours of straight studying; maybe they say that they want a job, but they refuse to stop using drugs to pass a drug test. While many of these habits hold you back, they fulfill a purpose—they make people feel safe. People are content with the familiar. Day after day, people carry out the same patterns. The future becomes predictable. Therefore, if habits make your reality, and you want to change your reality, then the answer is simple: you have to change your habits.

Developing a delayed-results mindset is challenging; many people get caught up in an environment that doesn't encourage new habits. It's tough when we're constantly pummeled by forces pushing an immediate pleasure-seeking mentality, whether it comes from your friends who want to get high today, a program focused on getting you an immediate job, or a weight-loss plan that promises ten pounds down in two weeks. The redundancy of these efforts is a powerful force weighing against your success because it is exactly the opposite of what you need to make it: a delayed-return mindset.

Take Ali. Each morning, he promised himself that he would go out and find a job, yet he greeted each day by scrolling through all of his social media pages for a quick dopamine hit (that natural chemical that floods your body and makes you think you're happy). When he *did* roll in to class, he would spend 60% of his day looking at his phone or daydreaming about the wicked game of Fortnight waiting for him. He'd head home, abandon the idea of homework, and spend the night switching between video games and social media. In bed, he'd promise himself that he'd go out and find a job the next day only to wake up and repeat the same routine, day in and day out.

Any transformation from your old self to your new self will feel uncomfortable (even threatening) to anyone who's been trained to seek out instant gratification. Our culture has trained us to be that way: educational systems emphasize passing the test, workforce systems stress landing the job, and so many healthcare systems focus on simply doling out quick-fix medications for symptoms instead of solving the root disease. Investing in the long-term isn't yet a focus of the world you move through, but don't let that fool you: a delayed-result mindset is what is required to truly survive and thrive in it.

MAKiN' iT isn't defined as just getting and keeping a job or going to college—that's only thinking about the short-term. MAKiN' iT is about adopting a delayed-results mentality to achieve goals and reach opportunities you may have never known existed, and it begins the moment you start consistently taking responsibility for your life, freedom, and Future Economic Opportunity (from now on, we'll just call that "FEO" for short), and helping others do the same. And when we say *future* economic opportunities, we mean it. Despite what social media would have you think, the ages of fourteen to twenty-six aren't your financial-building years. Instead, they're laying the stepping stones for economic opportunities down the road, paving the way for good jobs and successful careers. In a recent report out of Georgetown University, researchers found that back in 1980, young white adults reached the middle wage of their careers at age twenty-six, and young African Americans reached it at twenty-five. Nowadays, those numbers have climbed to thirty and thirty-three, respectively.[1] What that means for you is that it takes longer to climb that ladder now than it did before.

Gaining traction in the labor market takes time, and unfortunately, it takes longer for some than others. If you want to start building that FEO for a brighter tomorrow, you have to start today and be consistent in your efforts to get there, taking advantage of every opportunity that ambles your way.

Doing something once—or even once a day—isn't enough. Instead, take as many steps as you possibly can each day, exercising that mental muscle, until pushing for what will positively impact your life becomes habit.

1.2. Stuck

Do you know how many young adults between the ages of sixteen and twenty-four aren't in school or working right now? One in eight. That's roughly 4.9 million[2] disconnected youth who are potentially facing poverty, substance abuse, early pregnancy, violence, and undiagnosed or unaddressed mental and physical health problems. Millions more in the workforce or school are barely holding on with nothing to look forward to beyond low-wage, punch-clock jobs, and cash-sucking educational programs.

However, social media feeds us a different picture, one ripe with images of attractive, carefree young people living picture-perfect lives through a filter. Don't be fooled. In reality, a lot of young adults are seriously struggling. These vulnerable souls are disconnected from the people and resources they need to succeed, and because of this isolation, many get caught up in street life and don't manage to make it out alive and free. Those lucky enough to make it out in one piece often had to navigate a dangerous, unclear path to get there.

Chances are this all sounds familiar—you might even be reading this now still thinking there's no hope—but the fact that you're even going through this book should show you there's plenty of hope because you're dedicated to switching up your situation. You're already living Universal Success Habit One: successful young people consistently make moves to advance their lives, freedom, and FEO. As you work your way through this book, you'll begin taking the steps needed to make this habit a daily part of your own life and tap into the success it brings.

Remember: this isn't a game. This is your life. Now's the time for you to wake up and start becoming your own master.

You ready? Let's do this!

1.3. True Survival

How many times have you heard someone justify doing things that promote death, incarceration, and unemployment as a means of survival? Have you ever stopped to wonder: if the result of their actions is jail time, death, hurting someone else, or staying unemployed (or underemployed), how exactly is that survival?

Think back on all the times someone has given you misleading survival advice. You know the kind. Stuff like, "It's not illegal if we don't get caught," or "I'd rather be judged by twelve than carried by six." How many times has someone has told you something like "snitches get stitches, money over bitches" or "if you love me, you'll do it?"

We'll level with you. People don't share this kind of advice to help you grow; that advice only keeps you down in the mud. This misleading survival advice isn't just coming from your peers—it comes from just about everywhere, including corporations that boast a nondiscrimination policy when 50% or more of their new hires are found through current employees. Misleading advice creeps out from behind government programs that promise jobs and careers when they are unequipped to handle the host of social, economic, and physical needs that people face. Community colleges or universities swear they have financial aid yet lack the resources to help first-generation college students navigate and secure the funding they need. You can see this misinformation all the way down to ads: how many times have you seen an Instagram post or billboard promising joy, love, or cash, if you just drink the soda or buy those shoes? In all these cases, people and businesses are looking out for their own, immediate survival—not yours. Companies and programs like those are always hustling for their next dollar or business deal and see people as disposable numbers.

Even in well-meaning circles (such as programs or mentors meant to help you), adults can spout misleading survival ideas that keep young adults down. In our thirty-plus years working with communities, we've heard teachers asking, "Why should a kid go to school when they can make thousands a week on the street?" We've overheard youth workers romanticizing death and disrespect through their music choices in the presence of young folks knees-deep in the violent reality of those lyrics. It's uncommon for teachers and youth workers to receive any training on how to counter these misrepresentations. Many use these ideas to shift the blame off of their own shoulders when they fail to do their jobs. When we start training sessions with youth service workers, we always kick it off by asking them, "What misinformation leads your students away from success?" The answers pour in: "They believe they should get everything now." "They'd rather smoke weed than get a job." "They're too hung up on looking cool." "They don't want to work for anything." These youth workers are full of answers then, but when we ask these same professionals how much time they spend addressing these misrepresentations, the room gets quiet.

What we try to tell them is this: if you have someone trying to get somewhere and their map is all wrong, don't waste time teaching them how to read the map; give them the *right* map. You may have started this book with the wrong map for success, but together we're going to draw out the right one so you can identify, address, and redirect all the misleading survival advice flooding you and your community.

The big question is when did all of this misrepresentation start?

1.4. The Origin

Power

Power is the degree of control people or groups of people (including corporations and Uncle Sam) have over the systems, resources, and laws that affect others.

Power isn't as cut and dry as it seems at first glance. It can be teased out into three murky layers: visible power, hidden power, and invisible power. **Visible power** is the stuff we see day in and day out: our government, explicit laws, the military, and other authority figures. These positions are held by people who uphold laws that benefit themselves, even if their wants and desires don't benefit the majority. For example, consider how many medical organizations are run by men. Even though half of the population could get uterine cancer (or similar illnesses of the reproductive organs), research for those diseases is under-funded because of the gender gap in medical research. As long as people at the top can't understand the diverse needs of their community, certain groups of people won't always have their needs met.

The problem isn't the streets – and it isn't hip hop either. People are all too eager to point the finger at popular culture, drugs, or fashion. What they don't see is that these are symptoms of the real problem: power, privilege, and injustice.

Unlike visible power, **hidden power** isn't something discussed explicitly. Hidden power concentrates on the idea that certain people are behind the scenes, pulling strings on what makes it to the congress floor or what comes up for debate in a corporation. This kind of decision-making from the top impacts the information that regular joes receive since certain topics are deemed more newsworthy than others. Hidden power makes it harder for social issues to gain footing in the news if none of the people holding the cash are making noise about it in the first place.

Murkiest to identify and even harder to sway, **invisible power** can be found in our day-to-day lives. It boils down to ideology: the beliefs and sets of values placed on cultural norms that keep people upholding these kinds of values in their daily life regardless of whether these norms and values benefit or harm them. It's like being born into a family that doesn't have a lot of money. Chances are if you were born into a family like that, you were fed limiting ideas of what you were capable of from day one, right? Teachers, family members, and your community weren't pushing you to be the next Barack Obama or Ellen DeGeneres; however, people at the top give their children the resources and empowering language to reach for the stars.

Head spinning yet? Buckle up, there's more. These three layers of power operate on two different levels: **the micro** (personal, immediate circles, families, and communities) and **the macro** (government, corporations, and religious institutions).[3]

What systems have impacted your MAKiN iT journey? Write a system in the first column (for example, you might write education, criminal justice, major corporations, the government, or the media). Next to it, write down who makes the rules or laws for these—it can be either specific names or just descriptions of the kinds of people in charge. In the third column, jot down ideas for how you can influence those rules, and then share a step you can take to be the one in power instead.

 Make the Move

System	Who makes the laws?	How can I influence this system?	What can I do to be the one in power?
Ex. Education			

Privilege

Privilege is something of a buzzword these days, flitting around news articles and Instagram posts. Privilege refers to the benefits and easy living that groups receive for being in power. It could be a benefit (like being a white man and earning more money than any other group of Americans) or an exemption (like being straight and never having to worry if someone will harass you for taking the person you love out to dinner). There are many kinds of privilege, and we all benefit differently at different crossroads.[4]

An example of privilege that a lot of Americans don't even consider is straight, cisgendered (meaning you identify with the gender you were assigned at birth) privilege. Take a teenage trans* man, for example. Just walking through the world as himself, he's on the receiving end of harassment by his classmates, often unable to use the bathroom for the gender he identifies with, and lives in a body that doesn't line up with the image of himself in his heart. Even for young trans* people whose parents are supportive, many states make them jump through hoops to get the medication they need, which can lead to academic hardship, depression, or even suicide.

But privilege goes beyond sexual orientation. The problem isn't with the people struggling; the problem is with the systems in place designed to keep the folks already down from looking for a way out. It's a problem when people who are homeless are punished for sleeping on the streets (ike in Colorado, where the fine for sleeping is either ten days in jail or $250. All that does is slap folks with criminal records and makes it harder for them to get off the streets.[5] These are just two ways our culture continues to give misleading survival advice, leading young people down the path that ends up nowhere.

Let's look at your own identities, compared to the people in power. Chances are that you'll be at an advantage in some places and a disadvantage at others. That's okay—most people are. In the column beside each section, write down the way you identify yourself. In the column beside it, write down how you think others perceive you based on each identity, for better or worse.

Make the Move

Identity Markers	The people in power mostly are...	I am...	People think of me as...
Gender	Men		
Race	White		
Sexuality	Straight		
Religion	Christian		
Wealth	Rich		
First Language	English Speakers		
Physical Health	Fit		
Mental Health	No mental health problems		
Physical Ability	No disabilities		
Body Type/Size	Slender/Athletic		

Injustice

Injustice, the final facet of the origins of our struggles today, is all about unfairness or undeserved outcomes. It's the way that some people get punished hard for things that others only get slapped on the wrist for. It happens far too often that when people seek power, they wield privilege, jumpstarting a cycle of pouring injustice onto the people below them. This applies anywhere and everywhere. Just think about what happens if you're jumped in a part of town filled with blue-collar workers (police are generally not as helpful as if it had been in the rich part of town).

Look around your social circle and community and think back to the privileges and identities you wrote down earlier. What injustices have you seen in your community or with your identities that the folks from the more privileged identity wouldn't experience?

_____

_____

_____

When you think about survival, what phrases come to mind? "I gotta do

1.5.   Resetting for the Long-Term

what I gotta do!" "My family has to eat!" "I can't just let her disrespect me like that!" Have you heard anyone use statements like these to justify their actions, behaviors, or values? Was that person you?

Defining survival is ambiguous, open to more than one interpretation and prey to double meanings. According to the Merriam-Webster Dictionary, survival is "the act or fact of living or continuing longer than another person or thing." But what does that mean for you? If you're defining survival relative to the person down the street, and your goal is to go to jail or end up dead later down the line than they did, then you've only got your eyes on your short-term survival. Often, this kind of outlook shows up in our financial decisions and economic opportunities. If we're stuck on making it only from one rent check to the next, it's hard to see the path ahead to true survival—the real way out, free from jail, death, or financial troubles.

A lot of young people misunderstand survival this way, defining it as the things that promote their death, incarceration, and long-term underemployment or unemployment. For example, take a young man who dealt drugs to get money. In the short term, he was looking for ways to feed his baby daughter, help his girlfriend out, and keep up with his mom's bills. Without a diploma, he thought dealing made sense; in his point of view, how else could he keep up with all those expenses? Eventually, however, his lifestyle caught up with him, he got busted, and ended up in jail. Because money had never been a sure thing for him, he had to settle for a public attorney instead of hiring a highbrow lawyer. His short-term vision of survival landed him in prison for the long haul.

People weren't meant to do things that contribute to their demise or the demise of their children, so why do so many people buy into these dangerous narratives? For the answer, we need to dig into our ancient roots.

When our brains developed the way they are now, the landscape looked different—we're talking 200,000 years ago different. Because of this, our brains evolved to work under the needs and stressors of a prehistoric landscape—the kind of landscape we've been calling "immediate-results," and what scientists called "an immediate-return environment." Back then, our problems were all centered on the moment. If we were hungry, we ate. If there was a storm, we found shelter.

In the past five hundred to thousand years, though, our world underwent a massive shift. Now, most of society operates as a "delayed-return environment." How well we do at work impacts getting paid in a few weeks or at the end of the month. Eating healthy in your twenties saves you from health problems in your fifties. Putting in the work at school translates to a brighter future five to ten years down the line. And it's a lot to expect young people who grew up in financially unstable or food-insecure homes to work around their mental conditioning and plan for the fall future. After all, it's hard to think about being able to afford a comfortable living situation one day when you have spent your whole life knowing the stress of not being able to pay the utility bill.[6]

According to a study done in the Netherlands, this ability to shift your mindset to a delayed-return environment is much easier if you aren't under the thumb of power, privilege, and injustice.[7] Imagine a person whose parents have always footed the bills, a person who was given a chance at anything he ever thought about trying. At sixteen, his parents bought him a new car, and at eighteen, he applied to colleges without worrying about how to cover tuition. When he graduated, he knew his parents' friends would be there to connect him to his first job. Planning for the future and looking ahead was easy when he never had to worry about how to pay his bills in the meantime.

The biggest issue here is that privileges aren't extended to all of us equally. Instead, many people have to burn at both ends to even reach stability. Hardships blur the line between true survival and those misrepresented survival techniques you've been fed. All too often, we get stuck in the mindset of getting our bills paid or food on the table "by any means necessary."[8] Often, that leads young people to dropping out in the name of making a quick buck. Hustling opportunities replace legit jobs because pay is immediate. And when a better tomorrow doesn't seem to be coming, it's all too easy to grow focused on the now, especially when systems of privilege, power, and injustice are only misinforming you, promising you're right.

But if you shift your thinking to how hard work could pay off in the next year, beyond just the next few weeks, you'll tap into true survival— and the path to really making it. When you look at Maslow's Hierarchy of Needs[9]— a pyramid chart that shows the order in which humans' needs must be met—it makes sense that some people find themselves trapped in the mindset of immediate returns. If your basic needs of safety, stability, and food aren't met, it's a massive shift to even start looking at how to reach self-actualization—pursuing your dreams and stretching out to thrive.

It takes work. Developing a true survival mindset—one that isn't afraid of looking head-on at the long-term—isn't easy, but it *is* the best way to guarantee you'll make it. Research has come out in recent years showing your brain is flexible; new connections are constantly being made, and if your brain so much as believes in its ability to improve, then it will.[10] Think about that—just knowing you can do it, believing in your ability to adapt, is key to your success. And it doesn't cost you a nickel. All it takes is a shift in how you think of your brain. Like working out any muscle, it'll take time to see results. You can't just think of the future once and consider yourself done. There will be setbacks along the way, just like a bad day at the gym. Just remember that one hiccup doesn't launch you back to square one if you keep on training your brain to look at the long-term. You've got this—one step at a time.

1.6. The Contagion

Once you realize you've been swallowing a false survival mindset, you'll feel like you woke up from a long and delirious fever, but when you look around, others are still moving through the self-destructive motions you used to, and you'll find yourself questioning why people in your circle are still so deep in it.

The answer is survival contagion, the rapid spread of misinformation that insidious habits help you survive, disturbing people's true life, freedom, and FEO. The folks spreading the contagion of false survival information are misrepresenters, and if your social circle is made up of people deep in the survival contagion, it can be hard to yank yourself out and onto the path toward success.

This survival contagion crops up in many ways. Take the screwface, for example. That angry or unsmiling expression so many young people put on as they move through their day—how do you think that messes with your FEO? In 2016, three thousand people answered a survey about how they found their job, and the results were overwhelming. Over 80% of people who responded said they found their job through connections.[11] Essentially, it's less about what you know or who you know, and more about who knows you and likes you that lands you your jobs. Think about that screwface you're putting on. If everyone is intimidated, how will people get to know you, trust you, and want to hire you? That screwface could be contributing to your economic downfall. We're not telling you to start skipping around the hood with a cheese grin and throwing out daisies, but we are telling you to check the survival contagion and question what it teaches you.

A sneak preview, watch what we do and what the hood teach you."

- Rakim

Thumb through a hip-hop magazine and then through a business one. Count the number of smiling faces in each. What do you see? Grimacing or stone-facing might be considered cool, but is it going to help you pay the bills? Trust me, you're going to have a hard time convincing an employer to hire you if you're walking around like you've got beef with the world.

What makes you put on that screwface in the first place? Showing a lack of enthusiasm as a way to be cool weasels its way into your social circle until even looking uninterested at school is "in." What more clear-cut example of immediate-returns mentality is there than not wanting to seem interested in school because your crew has decided it isn't cool? The friendships you're wrapped up in now probably won't be around in ten years, but those bad grades from the days when you were trying to impress people by skipping class and giving the teacher grief are there for a lifetime.

If this all sounds too familiar, you're starting to think about getting out and moving on to a group that promotes your true survival, but it can feel hard to drop your current friends and seek out people with your best interests in mind. We're social animals[12] and our lives revolve around building connections with others.[13] Once we slide into a social group, it takes a lot of willpower to pull ourselves out and into another group, and when young adults do leave a social circle that was sick with the survival contagion, their old friends feel insecure, unsure, and hurt. And intentionally or not, they don't want you to succeed because of that. They want you back in their group. When you try to talk about your drive to thrive with your crew, they may try to put you down or make you scared of heading out into that unknown. All you can do, though, is keep moving forward toward success, and hope they see you as a streetlight showing them the way out too.

1.7. Redefine Survival

Most people have a mixed-up understanding of true survival. People whose build their survival code on trial-and-error will always lose out to those who learn from watching others. Countless people have walked a road remarkably like the one you're on now. Repeating the mistakes of those who came before you won't yield any better results, so instead of mirroring what you've seen around you, learn from what's gone wrong. Think about what you've seen people do and figure out how to do it differently. Your life, freedom, and FEO depend on it. Failing on the same path so many others have gone down isn't progress; it's a self-feeding loop. Hurt repeats hurt. Poverty repeats poverty. Anger repeats anger.

In a society drowning in power, privilege, and injustice, these survival mistakes are just too costly – not only for you, but for everyone who looks like you. It's time you broke free. Let's work together to promote a new definition of survival and take the haziness out of what it really means to survive.

Start by identifying the misrepresenters in your life—the people giving you false survival advice.

 Make the Move

Has a friend, associate or family member ever try to justify a negative action, tool, belief, value and/or behavior as survival? Why?		
Name	False Survival Advice	Reason

Our lives fan out across two different worlds. The first world has positive connections: work, school, extracurricular activities, and church. Spending most of your time in that world leads to life, freedom, and FEO.

The second world is its dark mirror populated with dangers like drugs, gangs, alcohol, unsafe sex, crime, and dropping out. These elements pave the way to death, incarceration, and un- or underemployment. Because millions of Americans fall under the umbrella of the working poor (working paycheck to paycheck, unable to make enough to pull ahead), young people often get tangled in this second world, so eager to get fast cash that they willingly toss out their life and freedom to make a few dollars now.

These two worlds overlap for about 80% of the young people out there. Maybe they're going to school, but they're practicing unsafe sex, or perhaps they're reading books once in a while yet keeping destructive gang ties. They're on the basketball team but smoking a little weed on the side. On a scale of one to six, with one being entirely in the dangerous world and six being entirely in the world of your true survival, these people are somewhere between a two and a five.

Based on our observations and experiences in working with youth, it appears that only 15% of young adults are at that six, always doing things that promote their life, freedom, and FEO. That remaining 5% is trapped at the one, consistently promoting their own death, incarceration, and unemployment. If you really want to make it out there, you have to keep making moves and decisions that push you up the scale, towards that six—and away from the one.

There will always be forces out there trying to tip the scales one way or the other. The strength of the forces and your own willpower determine which way you sway. Surprisingly, most young people resist the forces dragging them toward the six more than the ones pushing them to the one.

We all are always reaching for that six, and we may never quite grasp it, but we can strive for it.

This survival scale is here to help you reflect on past decisions and inform future ones. By examining the impact of your actions on your true survival, you can take the ambiguity out of what it means to survival. With this scale in hand there's no room for misdirection or lies, leaving misrepresenters powerless. Most importantly, the survival scale is nonjudgmental; all your actions are degrees of true survival, and the power rests only in your hands. You are the only person with any authority to rate your actions, behaviors, and beliefs on that scale. It's easy to react to your own choices with regret and criticism. Instead, try using the opportunity to consider what you can do today to help you move up on the scale and which forces help or smother that success.

Make the Move

Choose a recent action or choice you made that concerns you:

_____

How would you rate that action on the survival scale?

_____

Why did you select that rating rather than a lower/higher rating?

_____

What would need to happen for your rating to move up the scale?

_____

How would your life be different if you moved up one degree?

_____

Now think about the information you're getting about how to survive: What's some advice you received recently?

_____

How would you rate that advice on the survival scale?

_____

Why did you select that rating rather than a lower/higher rating?

_____

1.8. Stages of Change

What sets successful young people apart from the pack is their dedication to their journey for life, freedom, and future economic opportunity and their dedication to finding people who want to roll with them on that path. It's not a matter of whether you're a leader or a follower. It's all about movement. Roy Rogers once said that even if you're on the right track, you'll get run over if you just sit there. If you're ready to fight the forces that are trying to suck you downward to the one, you have to put in the work—and nobody else can do it for you.

You already have the energy in you to make this happen, but we frequently sink our energy into all the wrong places. The trick is knowing how to redirect your energy toward that six.

What five things are forces of misdirection in your life—things that push you towards a one? Write the top five on the left, and on the right, jot down how many hours or minutes you spend doing this thing each week.

1. _____   _____

2. _____   _____

3. _____   _____

4. _____   _____

5. _____   _____

Now, what are five things you want in your life?

1. _____

2. _____

3. _____

4. _____

5. _____

Take a good look at that list of five. What are five things you could be doing to work toward what you want? Write them down on the left, then write down how long you think each activity would take per week on the right.

1. _____   _____

2. _____   _____

3. _____   _____

4. _____   _____

5. _____   _____

The time you need to make a change is there, but don't expect it to be as easy as an overnight shift. Real change evolves over six stages,[14] and knowing about them can help you figure out where you're at on the scale and how to move forward into the next steps of change.

1. Precontemplation

Since you picked up this book, chances are you're well past the precontemplation stage. On the survival scale, think about the precontemplation stage as a zero. When you're here, you might know on paper that your behaviors are dangerous and can land you either dead or locked up but have no interest in changing. By picking up this book and making it this far, you've demonstrated that you're moving past this stage and moving into the second stage.

2. Contemplation

When you're here, you're doing just what the name implies: contemplating how to make a change. You know something's gotta give. A lot of times, people in this stage of change can see themselves making the shift in the next six months. Maybe (and if you're reading this book now, it's likely) you're open to advice or are willing to figure out how to start getting ready. Maybe you haven't quit smoking yet, but you're seriously thinking about how you should. Maybe you find yourself listening extra hard to people when they're talking about how they quit.

At this stage, you're down to get information or advice on how to make the change, so it's critical that you let connections happen and observe the trial and error of others who've made the same change. In this stage of thinking about it, don't lose steam. Remember, the internet is a tool. This book is a tool. When you use them right, you're unlocking a treasure trove of information on how to make it—everything from how to nail an interview to how to tie a tie is out there, for free. You've just got to keep yourself open to the flow of knowledge.

If you really want to move to the next stage of change, the contemplation stage is a good time to start taking small actions, like watching YouTube videos or following more inspirational people on your social media. Maybe all you do is start daydreaming about what your life would be like—how it would be better—once you have that new lifestyle in your pocket.

3. Preparation

Once you have those foundations from contemplation, you're heading into the third stage: preparation. This stage is the trickiest of them all. When you're here, it's easy to lose confidence and waffle between here and stage two because you're gathering the tools you need to make the change in earnest. Inside of scrolling through the Instagram feed of someone who's making it, you're starting to seek out connections, programs, information, and resources that can help you reach that goal.

Knocking this stage out of the park boils down to one simple thing: confidence. And there's no easy way to go about it. The confidence to succeed in your goal depends on how prepared you are for it. Sometimes we're too scared to look the potential holes in our plans or weaknesses in our armor head on, but it's at this stage that it's so important to find any places we might fail. And when you find those potential hiccups, don't be discouraged. Instead, ask yourself how you can prepare for those pitfalls, so that if they come (and you know there's a chance they will), you'll be prepared to face them as you head into stage four.

4. Action

By the time you've reached this phase, you're beyond thinking about how your life will be once you have the change in the bag. At this point, you're working on your goals actively. Maybe you signed up for that class or dropped off your application. Maybe you've stopped buying weed or tossed your last pack of cigarettes. This phase is one of the longest, and many experts say it can take six months to really lock in this new version of yourself.[15] When you're here, the best thing to do is keep surrounding yourself with the things and people that promote your success. Even writing positive notes to yourself and sticking them on your bathroom mirror can help. Focus on avoiding the places, people, and things that encourage you to continue with the habits or lifestyle you're trying hard to move away from.

While this phase takes time (and is often the most difficult), persistence really pays off. One tip for making it to the next phase is to try and make these new habits a part of your social life and a core part of your identity. That way, you're walking through life as someone who's living the change you're seeking out.

5. Maintenance

Once you've been living in the change you embarked on for about six months, you've reached what's considered the maintenance phase. It may seem like your work is done at this point, but it's important that you stay awake, making sure a setback like illness, a breakup, or an unexpected bill doesn't push you back down to action, preparation, or even contemplation. But remember that when you get here, even if you have slip-ups, the guy who invented this idea of change (Dr. Prochaska) put it best: "the only real mistake you can make in changing is to give up on your ability to change."[16] Keep believing you can do it, and you won't be disappointed.

Believe it or not, maintenance isn't the end. If you want to really make it to that final step, you'll start to shift your thinking: obstacles or challenges will no longer be setbacks but will become opportunities to improve. You'll even be ready to take on more knowledge, skills, and challenges, but it takes time. You could be in this phase for years, but that time you put in is worth the decades ahead of you free, successful, and financially abundant.

6. Termination

Named like it is, this stage is the last stop. It's when the change no longer feels like a change but has become your new normal. At this point, the way you're doing things doesn't feel like work, and even the temptation to do what you used to is gone. Once you reach this stage, your change has become a part of you and is just what you do—not something you try for.

When you get here—and you have it in you to get here—you'll be surprised by what you're capable of and the new paths that are ahead of you.

All you have to do is take the plunge, and that starts by looking at yourself honestly, like you did when you named the five forces of misdirection in your life. We're going to take those and dive a little deeper, using a young man named Carlos as an example. He thought over his own forces of misdirection and identified five: weed, always missing school, social media, playing too many video games, and making excuses.

When you look at that list, it seems like small stuff, right? But when he was spending hours a day high and behind a phone or TV, things were out of hand, so he took a look at how he could shift his weed-smoking habits to help him get clear-headed and free.

Force of Misdirection	Stage of Change	What can you do to remove or cut back on the behaviors, actions, and attitudes that lead you to the problem?	What can you do that supports your effort to make a positive change?	On a scale of 1 to 5, how hard is it to make that change?
Weed	2	Cutting back from blunts to joints.	When I feel like smoking I can go to the gym with Paul instead.	2

Below, we have a fresh chart for you to fill out with your own problems. Think critically and ask yourself honestly – what is it you're able to start doing today? Right now? What's a change that's in your power? Little steps are okay, so long as you're heading towards that six.

Force of Misdirection	Stage of Change	What can you do to remove or cut back on the behaviors, actions, and attitudes that lead you to the problem?	What can you do that supports your effort to make a positive change?	On a scale of 1 to 5, how hard is it to make that change?

To keep improving – to really make it – you just need to increase the number of engagements and supports you have every day while maintaining what you started before. You got this. How can you get the ball rolling today?

1.9. The Awakening

What exactly does it take for someone to embody this new survival mindset and tap into the power to fend off the misrepresenters—to keep pushing towards a six? Often it takes nothing short of an awakening.

Why? Awakenings are powerful emotional moments, such as when someone gets shot or arrested, or when a person finds out they're unable to graduate. It could be the loss of a relative or significant other, or it could be the diagnosis of a disease. It's these moments that people realize what survival truly means and commit to making a change—at least for the moment. The problem with these moments is that they are fleeting. The effects last for a few days or a few weeks, but without the right support or perpetual awakenings, most people settle back into the situation that landed them there in the first place.

For many young adults like yourself, the event that sparked their awakening was tragic, like the death of a friend or family member. Others just got fed up with working low-income jobs or sitting at home playing games. For some, it was a legitimate fear of dying or going to jail. Whatever the reasons, most successful young adults had a moment where they looked around and said, "Something's gotta give!"

These powerful emotional moments rattle your cage and stir up the energy you need to push back against negative forces. We are energetic beings. When we're faced with negativity, our energy gets drained, until eventually our own vibrations turn sour, and we get caught in a loop of entrapment. But today you've decided you aren't going to sit around and wait to get shot before deciding to survive. Learn from others' mistakes and hold onto Universal Success Habit One. Keep pushing to the six. And remember: people who survive on trial and error will always lose to those who learn from others' trial and error. One of the time-tested ways that people awaken without a traumatic event is by surrounding themselves with positivity. Positivity raises your energy and vibration, refreshing you and helping you navigate the road to success.

1. Work out or be physically active
2. Be grateful. Think of all the good things in your life, no matter

how small.

3. Perform acts of kindness. Sometimes even a "thank you" can go a thousand miles.

4. Meditate. Close your eyes for ten minutes and focus on breathing. There are tons of YouTube videos to help you get started

5. Become aware of your thoughts and feelings instead of letting them control you.

6. Eat healthier and drink more water. Cut out the soda and energy drinks; sugar and caffeine muddy your thinking.

7. Spend time with positive people.

8. Be in the moment. Focus on the present – the way the floor feels beneath your feet, your breathing, or just observe what you see right out your window.

9. Clean up your room and organize your stuff. A cluttered space is just another type of negative energy weighing you down.

10. Unplug from devices. Shut off your smartphone or laptop and chill outside, take a walk, or read.

Conditioning and peer pressure can also lead to an awakening. Many young adults become part of groups that condition them to do things differently. Religions of all stripes are a great example. They spend a lot of time encouraging members to behave and act a certain way (usually compassionately). Think about the groups you're part of and ask yourself if the groups you're in are leading you towards life changes for the better.

From coast to coast, young people have shared the moment the lightbulb went off for them:

> *"I had moved to San Francisco from San Diego. I was on drugs and didn't even have a place to live. I moved to San Francisco to try to get it together but so far I wasn't. I worked in a skateboard factory and a grocery store. I later went to prison. I was out for six months and started blowing it again. It took a long time to make the change."*

— 22-year-old, San Francisco

"I started taking success seriously when I was in a shelter for single mothers. Their policy was that you had to do something with yourself—you couldn't just sit around and do nothing. So I found something to do; I saw a flyer about going to a program. Through my own motivation not to be on welfare, I finally saw the reality that I had to change."

— 23-year-old, Harlem

Surrounding yourself with positive forces is vital. Seek out supportive groups. You can even take it into your own hands and form your own MAKiN iT group at school or in a community center. All you need is five people to get started. When you finish the book, we hope you'll be inspired to join in on the movement. All you have to do is sign up for the MAKiN iT Nation at *www.edwardejesus.com*. Let us know what you're up to and how you're doing on your path.

If this book helps you grow, spread the word and build a community that works together to get up and out. Tell your friends and family, share it on social media. The work you're doing on yourself is powerful and it's something everyone can benefit from. Together, you all can move beyond simply wading through today's bleak reality and looking forward to the hope of tomorrow.

1.10. Awakened

What is it that successful young adults do differently? Once awakened, they enter a process of self-evaluation. Knowledge of self is one of the most powerful things you can possess. Self-awareness, or the consciousness of your own values, emotions, and character motivations, is a powerful tool in your personal development. By becoming more self-aware, you can take deliberate action in your life as opposed to just helplessly reacting to whatever is thrown your way. As you gain self-awareness, you may come to realize you've been impulsive before, unable to properly regulate your emotions, or unaware of factors in your environment that have derailed your progress. It also allows you to learn from your mistakes so that you don't make them again.

Remember that the process of self-awareness through self-evaluation can't take place without the right attitude. By adopting a positive mindset and building self-awareness through unflinching evaluation, you can figure out what hasn't been working in your life, get rid of it, and replace it with better habits—but it doesn't end there. To truly find success, you must be willing to continually evaluate your behaviors, attitudes, and values according to how well they promote your life, freedom, and FEO. Remember: life is a marathon, not a sprint.

Locked in a cell, you irrelevant – where all your friends go? You reminiscing how you was lit tho and balling out with them dudes that can't send pic tho. It was loyalty til it came down to them lawyer fees and indictments coming wit hockey numbers when you selling quarter keys.

- Meek Mill

UNIVERSAL SUCCESS HABIT TWO:

Successful Young People Consistently Build and Maintain Relationships with People Who Push the Six.

After nine months in Tucson, Eve had learned to keep to herself most of the time. Her father Ted had uprooted them from Salt Lake City after getting laid off. A fresh start, he'd promised. She kicked the gravel under sweltering heat and snorted. Yeah, right.

They had just pulled up in front of the latest apartment complex. Despite her phone promising it was only nine a.m., the Arizona sun beat down on their shoulders, the heat rippling off the sizzling pavement and warming the cardboard box she held in her arms. Ted led the way up the dilapidated stairs to their second-floor apartment. This was their third apartment in nine months. Ted looked at her hopefully as he crunched the key into the lock. "This is it! Home sweet home, baby." Eve mustered a smile for her dad, feeling as sorry for him as she did for herself, and went into the dingy apartment.

When they first moved, Ted had picked up a job at a fiberglass fabrication shop. Things had gone great—until his drinking problem caught up with him. He was handed his final paycheck after three months of showing up late and disheveled, beer already on his breath.

These days, he was balancing as many part-time gigs as he could scrounge together to keep a roof over their heads. Each move, they hunted for cheaper rent. Eve looked at the bare bulb in her bedroom ceiling. This time, they'd found the cheapest apartment in town.

High school wasn't much brighter than that bedroom bulb. She didn't know a soul and showing up in the middle of her sophomore year hadn't exactly made it easy. Back home, making friends hadn't been much easier. It had been like that since her mother passed away five years back. With her father either drunk or working, Eve didn't believe in stability and making friends. Instead, she buried herself in the one thing she knew wouldn't let her down: the internet.

Eve didn't bother meeting new people or joining clubs. Instead, she followed her favorite YouTube vloggers, practicing makeup off tutorials with clearance makeup from the drug store or diving through endless Snapchats, her earbuds blaring whatever artist had taken her heart that week. In this world, she didn't have to worry about not fitting in or finding friends.

Eve was weaving through the halls at school, neck craned over her phone, when her favorite Youtuber Liza Koshy's latest post got interrupted by a phone call. Eve's stomach dropped. Nobody ever called her. She picked up, and as a police officer laid out the news for her, she dropped to her knees in the hall sobbing. Her father had been driving to a job, drunk, and swerved into oncoming traffic, killing another driver.

The trial was swift. Charged with vehicular manslaughter, Ted was looking at four to ten years in prison. Eve was adrift, and without money to cover bail before the sentencing, Eve immediately got whisked away in foster care.

She was sixteen, and in her eyes, she'd already been alone for a long time before her dad's arrest. After being placed with a family, Eve sank into a deep depression. Here she was, hundreds of miles from her hometown, surrounded by strangers. The first family that took her in was nice enough, but Eve felt no connection to them.

Over the next two years, Eve bounced from home to home, doing the bare minimum to scrape through her classes before disappearing behind a screen online. She was on her phone so often that her vision started going bad and she got pounding headaches, but it never crossed her mind to stop. Why give up the only thing she'd ever been able to rely on?

It took her by surprise: her eighteenth birthday. Freedom! Ted was still in prison, but her birthday card from him arrived on time. As she read it, she cried. Here was her father, imagining her grown up and ready to conquer the world. These last two years hadn't made her any more prepared or confident. She knew she had to put on a brave face for her dad, but the truth was that the future terrified her.

She kept the card with her in her purse and set off looking for jobs. She went to every grocery store, fast-food restaurant, and shop she could find in walking distance from the transitional housing she was staying at. At the end of each day, her hand was covered in ink from all the applications she'd filled out. She kept it up for three weeks. Each application filled her with dread as she stared at the paper, aware she had no work experience or anything to fill those blank spaces with. After a month, not a single employer had called her back.

There was one person in Tucson that Eve had grown to trust: Sheila, her second foster mom and the only adult who seemed to get her. They both loved the same YouTuber (Liza Koshy) and used to talk over coffee for hours on the weekends. Eve had been so ashamed of her situation since turning eighteen that she'd been avoiding reaching out. But now, not knowing what to do, Eve gave her a call.

Sheila answered almost immediately, overjoyed to hear Eve's voice. Like any good friends, they picked up right where they left off, and Eve felt warm and safe listening to Sheila chat away on the other line. They caught up about the latest Liza Koshy video and how hilarious it was. The line grew quiet. Finally, Sheila asked, "How've you been, sweetie?"

As sudden as the tears that pricked the corners of her eyes, the words flowed out of Eve's mouth, telling Sheila about how hard it had been, about the endless applications with no call back. Eve was embarrassed to have been so upset on the phone and she tried to wrap up the conversation. "Anyway," she concluded, "I know you've probably got a ton of stuff to do. It was great talking to you!"

"Eve, wait!" Before moving to Arizona, she explained, she had been a youth advocate in Washington, D.C. Having been in the foster system herself, Sheila had wanted to give back one day. While learning the ropes in advocacy, she had come across a system for building something called social capital.

"What's social capital?" Eve asked.

Sheila told her that most jobs—between forty and eighty percent—aren't posted on job boards. What landing a job came down to, Sheila said, was who knew and liked you. "Social capital," she concluded, "ithe value of the connections we have with people, is the key to your economic opportunities."

For the first time since turning eighteen, Eve felt the foundations of hope bubbling inside her. "How do I even get started? I don't really know anyone." Eve moved a pebble around with her shoe as she stood in the shade outside of the store where she'd just dropped an application off.

Eve could almost hear Sheila's smile through the phone. "Sweetie, you know me."

Over the next few weeks, Sheila took Eve under her wing and filled her in on the foundation for social capital building, including the acquisition of work experience, skills, connections, credentials, and degrees. She talked to Eve about how to relate to adults, and the best ways to build and sustain those connections she makes.

Most importantly, with Sheila's help, Eve felt a bounce in her step. In the mornings, she was mindful of her appearance and started turning her phone on airplane at night to help her sleep better. When she showed up to apply for jobs, she approached potential employers with the best version of herself. In three months, she had connected with six influential adults, acquired her first job as a restaurant hostess, and even started making some friends. Six months later, Eve put down the deposit for her very own apartment.

Eve felt like a new person and her apartment made her proud. When she moved in, Sheila bought them two matching mugs, and she and Eve would have coffee together every week to check in. Eve started writing to her father more; he was going to be out of prison in the next five years, and she wanted him to have her success to look forward to. So, with Sheila's guidance, Eve laid the groundwork for furthering her education.

She had only barely graduated high school. Because she had spent so little time studying, Eve needed to brush up on most subjects. At around the same time she got promoted to being a server, she started taking weekend classes at a local community college, starting with math, before stumbling across some business courses that got her attention. Before she knew it, she had acquired enough credits to graduate with an associate degree in business.

With the associate degree under her belt, Eve wasn't about to let up on the momentum she'd gained, and she landed a scholarship to Arizona State University. When she started her classes, she was still waiting tables at the same place and had been working there long enough that they trusted her with big parties and the Friday night rush. At the university, she found herself swimming in a world of opportunity, surrounded by peers who were eager to succeed. Eve easily fell into a group of friends she could count on. At first, she wasn't sure what she wanted to study. After a year of trying out different classes, she finally found her fit: marketing. She intended to pursue a career as a social media manager.

Instead of wasting her youth glued to a device, shutting out the world, Eve found the courage to pursue a life that her father would be proud of. She had been through hell and back, and now she was standing tall, surrounded by friends and mentors who were pushing her toward success.

2.1. The Real Misrepresenter

Which way do you want to go?

Do you want to push towards that six—life, freedom, and future economic opportunity—or do you want to fall down towards the one—death, incarceration, and economic demise? The choice is yours, and there are folks out there who will help you make those moves, whichever direction you choose.

And it is a choice. It's not always about others influencing you; you could be the one doing the influencing. If you are praying, pushing, dragging, or walking others towards a six, salute! But if you're directly or indirectly leading others away from that six, it's time to wake up.

Maybe you picked up this book because there's a small voice inside of you, whispering about how tired you are of misrepresenting true survival to others. Do you have a little sibling? In all homes, no matter how rich or stable, little siblings look up to their older brothers or sisters, and sometimes, you're the only one who can show them the way. When about 200,000 youth are incarcerated each year, hundreds of thousands of siblings are left at home, thinking that the path to adulthood is behind bars.[1]

Are you a parent? Do you want your children seeing the kind of role model that Eve had in her story above, or are they worth more? At least 5.1 million kids in the U.S. have had a parent in jail or prison during their childhood.[2] You can either pile another number onto that statistic, or you can strive to give them a stable and happy childhood. That power is in your hands. Not having any kids or siblings doesn't let you off the hook if you're dragging others towards the one.

Close your eyes and visualize your mom's face, smiling. Then, once you have that, close your eyes again and picture her face when she gets all twisted up, on the verge of a nervous breakdown and unsure of how to make ends meet because of all the dangerous things you've done. Did she really have the bail or resources for your legal fees? Women (mothers especially) are bearing the brunt of these costs. While 63% of legal cases had family members footing the bill for court costs, 83% of those family members trying to help keep their loved ones out of prison were women. And it's not like the majority of these mothers, aunts, and significant others are made of money. The average court-related fines and fees are almost $14,000—almost an entire year's worth of pay if you're making $15,000 a year.[3] Does your mom deserve to bear the weight and financial burden of your mistakes?

Finally, picture the homie who's now picked up for some trouble you got into together. Did you ever visit him or send him those funds for commissary like you promised? Do you even take his phone calls? It's time you woke up to how your actions ripple out into others' lives.

Let's get real. Faking on survival has major consequences that don't just affect you. You have the power to make things easier for the folks you love—you just have to take those steps to change.

Let's look at a young adult we'll call Kat. Her mom has raised her alone since Kat's dad left when she was three, and as a teenager, Kat has started feeling salty. Why should her friends have the latest iPhone and trendy clothes while Kat's stuck with some hand-me-down Android and thrift store threads? Her mom works as a shift manager at the grocery store and closes most nights, so she doesn't notice when Kat starts shoplifting—until she gets caught lifting a new iPhone off the table at a Starbucks. Tapping into her small retirement she's been saving up for ten years, her mom springs to get Kat's fees covered. When Kat gets caught a second time, her mom doesn't have that money anymore, and Kat has to perform community service after a brief stint in jail. Kat's mom bends over backwards driving her to community service, and because of the demanding hours, her mom gets demoted back to a cashier. Out her retirement savings and with a degrade in pay, Kat's mom needs to pick up a second job to keep a roof over their heads—and all because Kat wanted to steal new clothes and a cell phone.

Do you mean to cause your family this heartache and financial stress? Maybe you don't even recognize the ways your actions have been ripping them apart.

If you're feeling sick thinking about it, there's a whole stretch of future ahead for you to make a change starting *now*. Take this opportunity to figure out how you've misrepresented success to the people that matter to you. In the chart below, write down three people whom you may have hurt by your actions. Really think about what you did that misrepresented survival, and figure out how you'd apologize to them. The first one is an example to help you get going.

 Make the Move

Who's been hurt by your misrepresenting survival?	What did you do that was misrepresentative?	What would you say if you could apologize? (Hint: say more than "I'm sorry.")
My little brother	I spent the night in jail after getting in a fight over some weed	"You're worth more than what I've shown you. Being a grown-up doesn't mean being locked up or being in fights. I'm sorry I haven't been the kind of role model you deserve."

2.2. Are You Representing?

Maybe you aren't the one misrepresenting but are instead the one trying to represent true survival, pushing others toward a six. You may be tired, feeling like you're the only one, worn down by all the negativity flung at you when you try and do the right thing.

Who said pushing the six was easy? You can't be a source of light unless you're able to endure the heat—but all that heat may not be as bad for you as you think. Have you considered that helping to move your peers out of the immediate-results trap is what's helping you develop your own delayed-results mindset? Turns out, giving social support benefits both sides of the interaction.[4] According to a 2016 study, when you give support, your brain fires up to help you reduce stress, which in turn helps you find solutions for improving your own life.[5] While pushing that six may seem like a lot of work, remember that the more you push it, the easier it gets to keep on going.

There are plenty of ways young people can help others in their lives push towards a six, including:

- **Peer mediation**
  Instead of throwing down for a fight, figure out how you can help two people solve their argument peacefully. At the end of the day, everyone will go home happier—and they'll have you to thank for it.

- **Civic engagement**
  The best way to break cycles of oppression, poverty, racism, and sexism that keep you down is by getting involved in groups that are working hard to make the world a better place for everyone.

- **Social entrepreneurship**
  Maybe you start writing inspirational hip-hop or join the slam poetry circuit. Use your voice to build community and spark conversations for change.

- **Volunteering**
Giving back not only helps the folks around you, but also lets you build your social capital and resume, to help you land that first big break down the road.

- **Teaching**
Leading presentations or workshops about the dangers of drugs, gangs, and violence. Teaching about your own experience is a powerful way to let others learn from your mistakes.

- **Tutoring or mentoring**
Accountability changes the courses of people's lives all the time. When you're working with someone else, you'll be invested in wanting the best for them, which starts with wanting the best for yourself.

- **Creating**
Don't sell art short in its ability to change culture. By making music, paintings, poems, or stories, you're adding a much-needed voice to the mix and empowering the creative community to make a bigger community impact.

With all of these, you get more than you give. Keep giving, and get creative. It's a sure-fire way to get yourself on the road towards the six. We spend a lot of time when we're down in that immediate-results mentality thinking about how to receive what we need, but now that you're armed with the knowledge that giving is a powerful tool for pushing you towards that six, consider it. What ways can you give?

In the chart below, write a way that you can be the one to give for each letter of the alphabet. For example, you could write "attending groups that pursue social justice" next to "A."

You've got this.

Make the Move

A	
B	
C	
D	

E	
F	
G	
H	
I	
J	
K	
L	
M	
N	
O	
P	
Q	
R	
S	
T	
U	
V	
W	
X	
Y	
Z	

Great work. That's twenty-six things—twenty-six! Which one of those twenty-six sounds the most exciting?

_____

Why?

_____

What are two things you can do this week to help you get the ball rolling?

1. _____

2. _____

2.3. Friends and Family

What do you do when the biggest misrepresenter in your life is the person who says "I love you" the most? It could be a mom who is overly critical and demeaning, or a dad who is an outright gangsta telling you to live the kind of life he isn't. Love shouldn't have such a sharp edge, and it absolutely should never push you away from true survival.

Not all successful young people come from stable and healthy families. What sets them apart is that while they love their families, they don't take the whole "I love you unconditionally" thing too seriously. There may be a lot of dysfunction pulsing through your family for reasons that have nothing to do with you. A lot of times, your parents' anger is masking their own guilt or unresolved pain, fear, and trauma. Remember, when trapped in the immediate-results landscape, people are looking to do only what solves their problems in the now. For your family, being angry can feel better than peeling away layers of trauma. Some people are more comfortable with anger because it's the devil they know, and seeking healing feels too far away.

Oftentimes, a parent or significant other may feel threatened when they see you trying to make changes for the better. Instead of being happy for you, they think you'll abandon them on your quest for success. They may undermine your journey in ways that you can't wrap your head around or make efforts to keep you in the situation they're in. Deep down, all families want the best for their children, but an immediate-results environment makes defining "best" hazy.

Never forget: it's not your responsibility to change your family. Therapists can help give you strategies to cope with family misrepresentation and the dangerous examples they set.[6]

Make the Move

Who are five people who lost their way?

Using the list above, complete this statement out loud:

[Insert name] **lost** their way. I **won't** follow. That's their today; it **will not be** my tomorrow.

Repeat this for each individual. Saying it out loud helps drive the message home. You've got this.

Now we're going to flip the script. Who are five people you know who are working towards that six?

Make the Move

Who are five people who found their way?

Let's take the time to pay homage to those people leading us to true survival. For all five, complete this sentence with their name, saying it aloud:

[Insert name] **found** their way. I **will** follow. That's their today; it **will be** my tomorrow.

It will be—you just have to keep on moving.

2.4. Switching up

With all these influences yanking at your ankles, it doesn't feel easy to push toward the six, does it? Real talk: most young adults switch up the game because they know they're about to get played, or that they're on a ticking time bomb. Anxiety is real. When you've been getting away with something a little too long, you can feel the hairs on the back of your neck raise, warning you that time is running out. It's nature's warning signal that something's about to go down.

This anxiety isn't a bad thing. Think of it as the fire under you that you need to keep up with this fast-paced world. The economy is changing, and employers are seeking folks with more skills. If you want a prosperous future, time's a-wastin.' You've got moves to make— you've been playing checkers this whole time without realizing you're in a game of chess. Think of the MAKiN iT community as your chess masters guiding you on which moves to make.

Remember, the immediate-results mindset wants you to feel like you need everything now, but true success lies in thinking in terms of delayed-results. Shifting that focus is vital. By age twenty-six, if you do the right things and work on staying alive and free and building up your future economic opportunity, the good things won't be far behind. Many of you readers are probably between 17 and 21. That gives you anywhere from six to nine years to make things happen. Think about how much you can accomplish in that timeframe. You can complete both college and snag a master's degree in that time. There's so much time left on your horizon.

If you're a little older, don't let that fool you into thinking your chances are up—you just have to work a bit faster. But before you worry, consider this: you spend about sixteen hours awake each day. Take away about four hours a day for eating and grooming, and you're left with twelve hours. Twelve. What are you doing with those twelve hours?

Make the Move

What ways do you waste your time?	How many minutes a day do you spend doing this?	How many minutes a week?

2.5. Do you have twelve inches?

Imagine for a second that each year of your life was a foot and that each month was an inch. If you're seventeen, that's 204 inches, give or take—204 months of your life. A lot has happened in those months, some of it better than others, and you've experienced a lot for your age. But all those experiences have brought you here, reading this book, ready to make a difference. Over those 204 months, there have been people, organizations, and institutions that truly wanted the best for you...and there have also people who've tried to drag you down.

Picture those seventeen feet in your mind. Your life. Now picture adding ten years—twenty-seven feet, 327 inches total. Each of those inches is a passing month. Really visualize that. What could you achieve and experience in those passing months ahead? What new skills, credentials, relationships, and friends could you gain?

Close your eyes and visualize your ideal future self. What do you sound like? Where are you? What are you doing? What are you holding in your hand? Once you have the image of your future self, listen to them—what is future you telling you now to stop doing? What is this future version of yourself urging you to start? Write down as many details about this visualization as you can. Try to use all five senses—it helps.

Now that you have that version of you in mind, picture another ten years. That's another 120 inches. Where do you see yourself in twenty years?

_____

_____

Thirty years?

_____

_____

Forty years?

_____

_____

Fifty years?

_____

_____

Sixty years? That's about seventy-eight years—seventy-eight feet stretching in front of you. Seventy-eight years is the average life expectancy for folks born in 2000[7]. That's 936 inches, or 936 months you have to make something meaningful of our life. To put that in perspective, 936 inches is about the size of a basketball court. One year (twelve inches) is about the size of a piece of paper. What kind of life and legacy do you want to leave behind when you pass on?

_____

_____

Let's do some quick math to see how many months you have left in your MAKiN iT journey. First, multiply your age by twelve to get the months you've lived so far:

_____ x 12 = _____

Next, subtract that number from 936 – the months in an average American lifespan – to see how many months you have in your life.

936 – _____ = _____

If you're seventeen, you have about 732 months left in your MAKiN iT journey. And your future self is really pulling for you to reach toward that six. Picture twelve inches again. That's one year. One year of your life to invest in a better future that, if we measured it in inches, is as vast as a basketball court.

And before you go thinking a twelve-month investment in your future won't pay dividends, reconsider: that twelve months can increase your income by a longshot. The wage increase is staggering. Young people can go from earning an average of $15 an hour to $20 an hour. You can go from a job with no benefits to full benefits, so the question you have to ask yourself is this: do you have those twelve inches?

Make the Move

What are some ways you can invest those twelve inches to build your FEO and push for the six?	What are some steps you can do this week (or even today) to get the ball rolling on these future plans?

2.6. It's Not Only What You Know...

There comes a point in every successful young person's life where they realize they have to stop hanging with the knuckleheads. Before you go pointing to a successful person you're sure still rolls tight with some knuckleheads, stop. These people don't exist—not in the long run—and if you see someone doing well for themselves but still rolling with the same people, know that it's only a matter of time before they either get themselves caught up in that immediate-results minefield again or they ditch the knuckleheads. You can't have it both ways.

Most successful young adults know the value of a positive connection with an adult or organization. It's the number-one asset for true success and the most common way people get jobs. Another thing successful young adults have in the bag is the habit of consistently building social capital—and not being afraid to spend it. Social capital is the value of your connections with individuals, organizations, and institutions. Research has proven repeatedly that young people with ample social capital do better in every aspect of their life, including finding gainful employment.[8]

Right now, you may not have many (or any) lifelines to the workforce. You may be held back by limited access to individuals who can expose you to different fields of work or help you thrive academically. It might be that you don't have people in your life who can help you counter the negative perceptions many people in the labor market and law enforcement have about African-American and Latino young adults. Maybe you're interested in enrolling in a credential program, but you don't know anyone who could help you put that hard-earned credential to good use. Without these lifelines, you're forced to face the working world alone, unsure of where to turn and without connections to basic information or opportunities for success.

If you do have those people in your life, you might not be connecting with them. For whatever reason, your relationships with the key people who could help you make it is tainted and sour. Maybe the problem is as simple as you only asking for help when you need it; research suggests that doing so puts the helper in an uncomfortable situation, making them feel like their arm's been twisted in a no-win situation, like they've been conned into helping you.[9] Guilt can also play a role. Maybe you're afraid that people you care about could find themselves in a worse situation by helping you.

Most young people, regardless of their employment or educational status, are connected to significant people who can help. One common problem is that you and your connections are in the same boat—or they might be ahead only marginally, keeping you from major social or economic leaps.

For instance, let's say you want to work in a local automotive dealership. Local contacts can help you do that, no problem. However, if you want to land a job with Tesla, there are some social gaps to leap over and some redundancy—repetition in your social circle's mentalities, abilities, and skills—to work past in order to overcome those barriers. With hard work and a little help from our book *Social Capital Building*, you can get there. For now, let's figure out how to lay the groundwork, and how to better spend the capital you have.

It all starts with learning to ask for help. There are many reasons why people don't ask for it: shame, guilt, not knowing what they need. Most of the time, people want to help you but just don't know how, or they're worried you aren't serious about using the help they might offer.

To get going, identify what kind of help you need in the first place. Do you need help finding a job? Getting credentials? Learning a new skill? Once you've figured that out, you're ready to make some moves.

2.7. Connections first!

Seek out the connection before getting the credential. When you have people in your life rooting for you, you can keep them updated on all the ways you've been improving your life, securing a reference to help you land meaningful employment and prepare you for those credential-building opportunities down the road. More than anything else, success hinges on who you know—not just what you know (specifically, it's who you know and who likes you). If the connections you've made so far have dismissed you as a knucklehead, don't worry. There's a lot you can do to change that—reading this book is a great first step.

Building social capital is not networking. Networking is an activity that doesn't always yield clear results. Building up your social capital, however, is an outcome. Unlike the idea of networking, where you're pounding the pavement seeking out folks who can help you, building social capital is reciprocal, built on five pillars:

1. **Compassion**
   This is a potential employer's awareness of the barriers in place, often systematically, to keep others from seeking out true survival

2. **Assistance**
   This is more nuanced than it seems. With true assistance, the person seeking assistance has identified what kind of help they need most, and the person looking to help has asked what they can do both. Assistance goes deeper, too. Think about what you know and have that can benefit employers and demonstrate it. This goes into the next pillar of building social capital.

3. **Reciprocity**
   Put your shoulders back. You may not realize it, but when you get hired somewhere, they aren't giving you a gift. You have a lot to offer in return and a lot to give, whether it's skills, insight, or an eye for design.

4. **Trust**

Learning to trust people who look, act, or sound different from you is critical – and an aspect of social capital that goes both ways. Show up as someone trustworthy and be receptive to others from different backgrounds as folks you can trust. The results may surprise you.

5. **Information**

What knowledge, ideas, or wisdom has your life taught you that could benefit your new connections? Do you have a fresh take? Do you know how to help something go viral? You have information worth sharing—and so do others. Listen to what people have to say and be willing to share the knowledge you have.

The MAKiN iT Nation is hard at work making sure both sides of the fence know about these pillars, called CARTI for short. We're working with employers and workforce organizations to give them insight on how to hire in a way that builds bridges, not barriers.

If building social capital seems like the way up and out, why isn't it being taught in schools and colleges? Why is it that teachers are more caught up with measuring what they think you should know rather than who you know? It's a blend of misinformation, undervaluing of social capital, and oppressive systems at work.[10] Recently, however, studies have come out arguing for social capital as the key to school reform.[11] But these kinds of shifts take time. Instead of waiting for schools to overhaul and incorporate social capital into their learning structures, take the power into your own hands.

Social capital is the automatic parachute that keeps the rich kids from crashing when they jump out into the labor market or get wrapped up in illegal dealings. It helps counteract those negative stereotypes employers hold about young adults, especially young adults who don't look like they do. Building up social capital is the most important thing you can do, and it starts with simple connections.

Why? Because it's the number-one way people get jobs. Connections remain the top job source, flying past job boards like LinkedIn and Mindsetjobs. In 2012, a survey showed that 46% of people get jobs through who they know, while only 20% found jobs through job boards and only 14% found jobs through job agencies,[12] so the question is this: why would you divide up your job-seeking time any other way? You should be spending about half the time you're seeking jobs building up your connections, especially when you consider that 60%-80% of jobs are never advertised or advertised improperly.[13] How could you prepare for the job that changes your life for the better if you don't even know it exists?

Most young adults have it backwards, not even focusing on building up their social capital until they need a job. At that point, it may be too late. The economy is changing rapidly and the only way to be prepared is to get connected. Knowing people in the labor market will ensure that you get the best information about the relevant skills, credentials, and education you need to be a success—those connections can be the ones to help you get through the door.

Let's say you want to become a phlebotomist. While there may be loads of information on the internet about how to become one, it pales in comparison to the information that you'll get from someone who's already a phlebotomist. Those people could tell you all about the most reputable training programs that help phlebotomists land the best jobs, the best avenues to go through to secure a job, or the best-paying phlebotomy positions available.

The trick to these connections is that these adults have to like you. Nobody wants to help a knucklehead get a job, and given the media's portrayal of urban youth as predators, killers, and addicts, it isn't hard to see why so many adults are disconnected from young people. While this perception isn't your fault, it's on you to build the bridge that connects you to opportunities, starting with those adults. Remember, MAKiN iT Nation is working from the other side too. We're in your corner educating employers on the importance of connecting to young people. You're not alone in the fight, but you do have to show up to make the change. Most of the things that you can do to ensure your success cost very little or nothing at all. You can't go to the store and buy a mentor. You can't purchase motivation or a formula to combat negative emotions and attitudes—you have to work at it. But if you're serious about making it, you got this.

Don't undervalue your community as a way to start building

connections. If you live in a poor community, all that means is that the majority of people are either unemployed or underemployed. It speaks nothing to the morals, values, and work ethics of your neighbors. If you just look, you'll find many good things in your community that you may not know are there: role models of achievement, sacrifice, and perseverance are everywhere around you.

If gainfully employed people are few and far between in your hood, though, you still need to link up with people who have abundant careers. How? For starters, you have to hone those basic social-capital-building skills. Relationships with adults don't come easy, and it can be tough to navigate which adults truly have your best interests in mind and which are still pushing you toward the one like it's their full-time job.

When looking for an adult to help you on your MAKiN iT journey, look for three things:

1. Can this person relate to me and my circumstances?
2. Does this person really care about my circumstances? Will they commit to helping me in measurable ways?
3. How is this person qualified to assist me in my MAKiN iT journey? What actions can they commit to?

Think about places within walking distance to you, or think about people in your family. Maybe there's a corner store nearby with a manager or owner who works hard. Get to know that person. Ask them questions about how to succeed and build a relationship with them. Think about those five pillars of building social capital (CARTI) and how you can engage in a relationship with them that benefits you both.

Often, the drive to build bridges is held back by the immediate-results environment you think you're stuck in. It keeps you from reaching out to people who might provide you with the most economic assistance in the long run. It may be easier or a quicker turnaround to talk to someone who can offer you a one-time gig and some fast money, but will that help you a year from now? Ten years from now? Instead, look to the future— get that long-term mentality flowing and dive into the connections that can help you improve your circumstances. While landing a one-time money-making opportunity can be exciting, getting to know someone who works in the field you're interested in studying can help you identify how to make the most of your time and land the best job down the road.

Unfortunately, this same mentality can be found in the affluent, too. They don't have to put in the energy to build bridges because they've already been built for them. That means it's on you to lay the foundation. It might take hard work to get some positive adults in your life, but you have the tools to get there.

First, think of the things you have to offer potential employers. List five things—and get creative. Are you a wiz at social media? Do you know how to organize messy spaces? Do you have access to a community that the employer would benefit from knowing? Write them below.

1. _____
2. _____
3. _____
4. _____
5. _____

With these abilities in mind, remember that you are a valuable addition to the workforce. All you need to do is demonstrate that to potential employers.

2.8. It's All About the Hub

To get going on your MAKiN iT journey, you need to assemble a group of individuals who can be supportive and help you. This group will serve as your hub. The average person has about 611 connections…who each have 611 connections.[14] That comes out to a whopping total of 373,212 people, or the entire population of most medium-sized cities in the U.S.

But what can you do with 373,212 contacts? Short of the impossible task of reaching out to three hundred people a day for three and a half years, you're never going to reach them all. What this vast network should tell you, though, is that your potential for connecting is immense. The world is yours. Still, while you may strive for three hundred thousand social media followers, what are they going to do for you if your brain can't meaningfully categorize them and you never establish those connections?

There's a sociological theory that says your brain can only maintain meaningful connections with 150 people, five of whom are in your closest circle.[15] So instead of pushing for hundreds of thousands of peripheral connections, shift your thinking: it's not the quantity—it's the quality. The value of each connection depends on you hunting for the people pushing you toward that six.

That's what sets social capital apart from networking: it's not about the numbers. It's about that hub of quality connections in your network. A hub is kind of like an airport: they're major points that help you get from one part of the country (or the world) to another without having to drive yourself all the way through each connecting point between. Without these hubs, traveling would be a nightmare. Hubs are efficient, saving you time and resources so you can arrive as directly as possible. A social hub is no different. The secret to being a master at building social capital is learning how to leap across these great social distances with the least amount of effort and time, so you can connect with the people who would make the biggest impact in your life. Why take five or six connecting flights when you could get somewhere on two or less?

According to the Small-World Experiment conducted by Stanley

Milgram, we're all separated by only six degrees (or people) from anyone else in the world. You're probably linked to Barack Obama through six people or less. That means you know someone who knows someone who knows someone who…you get the idea. By only six degrees, you could be connected to anyone from the former U.S. president to a barista in India. The power of connections is vast, and it all depends on how you navigate the web of people in your life. You don't have to build a massive network; you have to build up social capital. It only takes a handful of people—and an even smaller number of connections—to reach our goals.

The right people in your hub should be ones that believe in your potential and bring something to the table for your success. Your hub members will help you gain information about available jobs, give you the scoop on career opportunities, and encourage your education. More than that, they should be more than your mentors—they should be your friends, too.

Through personal involvement and mentoring, members of your hub will illuminate the systems, processes, behaviors, and skills required in the workplace. Many young adults get limited career information (at best) from friends, relatives, and counselors. In order to make career decisions, you need the opportunity to explore and increase your knowledge in the fields you want to pursue and bolster those interpersonal skills to boot. The ideal hub members are candid and supportive, willing to share their own experiences, and accept you as you are. They're also willing to be part of a team working on one common goal: your success.

If you're looking for real change, stop sinking your time into useless pursuits, and instead focus on building up your social capital hub. You'll be rolling in results in no time. According to a 2008 study, young adults that were matched up with mentors in well-run programs like Big Brothers Big Sisters experienced significant benefits, like being 46% less likely than mentor-less young adults to use drugs and 27% less likely to use alcohol. The young people in those programs also said they were more confident in their ability to succeed and even received higher grades than other young people not in a program.[16]

Once you get going, you'll be surprised by how quickly your hub comes together. Most adults are eager to participate positively in a young person's life, and more professionals are recognizing how powerful it is to invest in future generations. Maybe they're looking to give back some of what's been given to them. It almost doesn't matter why—the fact is that there are people out there happy to serve on your board. All you have to do is ask.

So how do you get a hub going?

At least five adults and one successful young adult should form your hub. That young adult will be different from the others, since they're a peer you can relate to on a level you may find yourself holding back from other, older hub members.

Consider inviting someone from your church or temple, a teacher you respect, or someone who works in your neighborhood to join your hub. If you're struggling to think of five, start by picking out one adult who could work alongside you to locate other members. Once you've established your five, interact with each of them at least once a month in some way. Your monthly one-on-ones can take place on the phone if you can't coordinate a time to meet in person, but make sure you get some face-to-face time at least once a season.

After you've been building your relationships with your hub members for a few months, try scheduling a group call where all the hub members can talk about your development, but keep it short and sweet, wrapping it up within fifteen minutes.

These meetings aren't times for you to show up empty-handed, hoping to be given secret knowledge to success. You have to be prepared or else risk wasting your hub's time, damaging the trust you've been working so hard to build. To prepare, assess where you stand on your MAKiN iT journey and any barriers you may be encountering. Share examples of your successes and what you accomplished since the last meeting—report cards, self-evaluation forms, a list of places where you sent your resume, and community service activities are all great examples of what to include.

When you meet, ask tough questions and be as direct as possible in your requests for help. For example, instead of saying, "I need help finding a job," say, "I'd like for each you to give me the names of three individuals I can contact regarding possible employment." Believe us, your directness will be refreshing and appreciated.

Take time as well to pop in for informal meetings between you and your hub members. It's important to visit at least two hub members in person each month. Give them a call and let them know you'll be in the area and would like to drop by their office. When you visit, focus on strengthening your relationship. Talk about what they do and how they're doing. Ask questions. Learn about their business and how they got to where they are. People love the chance to talk about themselves, and by learning their history, you're strengthening the bridge between you two. If you can, take the time to meet your hub member's coworkers and set foundations for those connections as well.

Through any of these meetings, formal and informal, don't worry if a board member challenges you at some point. That's what they're here for—to help you improve yourself.

Make the Move

Who could be part of your hub?	What are some ways you can help them?	What are some ways they can help you?

If you haven't figured out many people to add to your hub yet, don't worry. Come back to this chart as you grow your hub and add to it. All it takes is that first member to help you get started.

If you want your hub to work, you must make it work. Stay in contact with your hub, call meetings to order, and be specific when asking for help. This is your team, and you're the captain. If you don't put in the effort to make the meeting work for you, you won't get what you want out of it.

As with any organization, your hub has rules and responsibilities.

Inform members of the expectations below before they sign up. At the end of this book, you'll find a job description for board members to help you pitch the position to them.

HUB Member Responsibilities

Friend
A hub member has time to listen and provide compassionate advice and help when asked. They are someone who notices the little things and knows the value of simple phrases like "I'm proud of you" when it comes to building your self-esteem. They must be someone who realizes that time is integral when it comes to building relationships.

Role Model
A hub member is someone who has had to overcome obstacles to enjoy a successful life and is willing to share them with you. This responsibility can be fulfilled in creative ways. Maybe a member takes you to work with them one day. Others can be role models with their mannerisms, ability to control their temper, or their positive energy. A hub member should share their own goals with you and always help when you're seeking ways to further your education or discover job opportunities.

Link to the Community: Link to Business
A good hub member is knowledgeable about the community and bold enough to find out any unknown information that will help you secure a job. Your hub members will need to know or learn who the community and business resources are and how to access them, sniffing out information and developing your community business network so that once you graduate or get certified, you can land meaningful and gainful employment.

2.9. Tales from the Bright Side

Victor never gave much thought about having positive adults in his life. He was too busy living it up to hear them and being caught spending time with older people was embarrassing.

All that changed after his arrest for attempting to steal a camera (he was seventeen at the time). While the court fines racked up, he contemplated the people who had used to reach out to help, like the mechanic who had encouraged him to try his hand at learning his own engine. If he'd only listened to people like that, he never would have found himself in jail, thousands of dollars in debt.

After his release, Victor called each caring adult up and told them what had happened. He was ashamed, he said, and knew it had been stupid. "Anyway. I appreciate how much you'd tried to help, even if I'd blown it." To his surprise, each adult he'd reached out to had been thrilled to hear from him and committed to continuing to help him. Immediately, one intervened in his court case, another helped him secure a part-time job, and they all encouraged him to complete high school and start community college. Now, Victor is twenty-three and works in a community organization that helps young adults. He's in his last year of community college and still actively keeps up with his hub.

Holding back your feelings may save you from others, but it will never save you from yourself.

- *Chance the Rapper*

UNIVERSAL SUCCESS HABIT THREE:

Successful Young People Consistently Build Positive Emotions and Manage Hurtful Ones.

It was a frigid South Chicago night. Ayesha, Malik's girlfriend, had just gotten off her shift at the shoe store and crashed on his couch. Between work and school, finding quality time together was rough. Mostly, it was just Xbox One or Netflix and chill.

They had been playing Call of Duty for about an hour when Ayesha leaned back against the couch. "Baby, I'm hungry."

Feeling his own empty stomach rattle, he looked over at her and smiled. She smiled back, melting his chilly insides. "My uncle's been going on about this hot dog joint called Fat Johnnie's Red Hots. You game?"

She tossed the controller onto the couch. "You're speaking my language!" Even though it was less than twenty degrees outside and snowy AF, they both agreed to roll to the spot. The sidewalks were slick with black ice, and what was supposed to be a twenty-minute walk turned into an hour. Ayesha and Malik could already smell the hot dogs and polishes a couple blocks back, their smell wafting over to their wind-chapped noses. They were salivating by the time they got to Fat

Johnnie's and saddled up in line behind five other people.

By the time they got to the window, Ayesha and Malik were ravenous and both ordered dogs with cucumber and tomato. They huddled together while waiting for their order—and then it happened.

"Yo! Damn girl, you thicc! Can I squish it?" a man hollered at Ayesha.

"Bruh, what'd you just say?" Malik's voice started to rise. Malik was clenching his fists so hard his knuckles were off-white. This dude had messed with his girl. Who did he think he was?

The man held both his hands up. "Just complimentin' yo girl. Relax, my dude."

Ayesha was pulling on Malik's arm. "Come on, let's just wait for our dogs, k? Please?" He heard her voice tremor, but it was too late. The man had sauntered up to the counter to order, oblivious to the fury bubbling in Malik. When he turned around, all he saw was Malik's fist flying towards his face.

Punch after punch, Malik didn't hold back. He heard Ayesha screaming and was aware of several pairs of hands trying to pull him off, but he only stopped when he ran out of breath, the man lying on the ground limp. Malik glanced up, his breath making clouds in front of him, taking in the blood that had spattered dark against the snow and the side of Fat Johnnie's stand.

His hand found Ayesha's and they took off running, sirens blaring not far away. They got back to his apartment, still hungry. Ayesha wouldn't look him in the eyes, and after a few minutes, she mumbled an excuse and went home. This wasn't the first time he'd lost his cool, but the next day she stopped him at school, leaning against his locker.

"Can I talk with you?"

His stomach dropped, sure of what was coming. She held her books across her chest like a shield and in the back of his mind a voice whispered that she was afraid of him. His face felt hot.

"I love you, so so much. It's just—this," she gestured to the ground and he knew she was talking about the man sprawled out on the pavement. "It's too much." She looked him in the eyes. "We're done. For me— we gotta be." Wincing, she glanced away. "You're like your dad when

69

you do that. And I can't have black eyes in my future." She peeled her shoulder off the locker. "Bye, Malik." He watched her stooped shoulders as she walked away and punched the locker in frustration.

What smarted the most was that she was right. Violence wasn't new to him; it was all he knew growing up. His dad Terrance had smacked around his mom on the regular when he was little, and sometimes Malik had been the focus of Terrance's anger. Over the years he'd developed a speech impediment. Even now, he didn't talk much, especially not to new people. The only people he trusted not to laugh at his stutter were Ayesha and one teacher, Mr. Carlton. Now Ayesha was gone.

For the next week he stayed low key and away from the block with Fat Johnnie's. Graduation was coming up that summer—not that Malik was excited, but he didn't want to totally blow it. He spent most of his free time smoking herb and playing Xbox One, burying his feelings in a haze of smoke and games.

One day after English, Mr. Carlton stopped Malik on his way out to talk. It was Malik's last class of the day, and they'd become tight after Mr. Carlton had shared his love for hip hop, particularly Chicago's finest. The two loved talking about their favorite artists, like J Dilla, Common, Kanye West, and Lupe Fiasco. Mr. Carlton had grown up using MPCs to flip samples. Now, Malik liked to enlighten him about current trends and the latest equipment, like the Maschine Studio.

The past week, though, Malik hadn't wanted to talk with Mr. Carlton, and Mr. Carlton had picked up on it. Something was bothering Malik— his stutter was usually more pronounced during those times—and Mr. Carlton kept him after class to catch up. Eventually, Malik admitted that Ayesha had broken up with him. That much Mr. Carlton had guessed. There was something else though, something deeper, so Mr. Carlton kept him talking, asking about the breakup.

Malik looked down, scraping at a piece of tape on a desk with his thumbnail. "I don't know, man. I've got this anger problem." Once the words were spoken, Malik couldn't seem to stop, opening up about Terrance and his past. "I don't wanna become my dad," he finished.

"That's not going to happen, Malik. You're here now, showing you care, right?" Mr. Carlton leaned against the edge of a desk and told

him about different techniques for handling emotions. He ran through a few different ideas, nothing clicking with Malik until he suggested meditation. He took in Malik's raised brows. "Hear me out, Malik. With meditation, it's just focusing on your breath. Taking that time to be in the exact moment you're in—and only that moment. Hard to be angry when all you have to do is think about your breath."

Malik figured he didn't have much to lose, so he let Mr. Carlton send him a few videos on meditation. But he knew Malik needed more and took a chance, offering to introduce him to a friend that worked at a local youth health clinic. "You got a minute? We could go there now."

Malik wanted to say no and go home and get blazed, but he thought of Ayesha, that man's blood on the snow, and his own dark room with his Xbox. "Yeah, man. I got time." They walked over to the health clinic to meet Mr. Carlton's friend, Frank, who specialized in anger management.

When they got there, Frank was easygoing with a wide smile. Within thirty minutes, he'd convinced Malik to join a program that had just started up, something called "motivational interviewing." It was a type of client-centered counseling, Frank explained, focused on addiction and anger. Malik wasn't too sure, but when he went to his first session the next day, he was surprised by how friendly everyone was, and how much they genuinely wanted to help out.

But no matter how nice everyone was, the first couple weeks were rough. Malik was facing memories he'd buried years ago, like watching his mom thrown down a staircase, Terrance's hand raising to hit him again and again, being bullied for his stutter in the third grade.

Malik persisted in therapy, knowing this was his one shot to free himself from his past. After several months, he felt like a new person; for once in his life, his head was clear. Whenever he did get angry, he knew how to cope and let it roll off him. The days of losing control or hitting strangers was behind him. Still, as graduating loomed two months down the road, he felt lost. Sure, he was proud to have pulled the grades to make it, but he didn't have any vision for himself down the line.

One day after class, he asked Mr. Carlton for advice. "Well, Malik, that's something we all wrestle with at some point. You just gotta find your 'why' or your purpose. Everything else will clear up from there."

Malik didn't really understand what Mr. Carlton was talking about, but as he was walking home, with Kendrick Lamar in his ears, the answer washed over him. That "why" was music. When Malik got home, he started applying to jobs, using Frank and Mr. Carlton as character references.

He got hired within a month at a music store, and he spent the following six months saving up for equipment. Eventually, he could afford a used MacBook Pro, some FL Studio recording software, and a Maschine Studio production system. When Malik wasn't at work picking up extra shifts to save up, he spent every spare minute learning the ins and outs of making stellar hip hop beats.

After a year, Malik came across an online remix contest for one of his favorite artists and decided to throw his hat in the ring. He was ready. By the week's end, he uploaded his entry.

A month passed, during which Malik checked his email on his phone obsessively. One morning before work, he checked again, and there it was. He won first place! The prize included $25,000 and the chance to produce an all-original joint with the artist.

A new emotion welled up in Malik, one he was proud to embrace: undampened joy. Tears of happiness pricked his eyes, and he shot Mr. Carlton and Frank a quick "thank you" text for believing in him. Because he could control his emotions, he'd been able to funnel that energy into his passion: music.

3.1. In your feelings

One thing that sets successful young people apart from the pack is their dedication to regulating the emotions that lead them towards the one. They've learned the dangers of them and take active steps to keep them in check and build up positive ones. Refusing to let a burst of emotion mess up their future success, they face their feelings head on, day by day, step by step.

It's vital to support yourself emotionally on the regular. Managing your emotions and integrating techniques like Malik did is how you're going to succeed on your MAKiN iT journey. Like bodily fitness, it's not just genetics that determine our success: it's our environment, our social circle, our diet, and our access to resources and places that make the difference. Knowing and acting on this makes the difference between getting into shape or not. Mental strength is no different.

If emotions like anger can lead us away from that six, why have them? Like that immediate-results mentality, it has to do with our ancestors. We spent hundreds of thousands of years relying on anger and fear to focus our attention and keep us alive. Eons of evolution have trained us to respond to rumbles in the bush and immediate things we perceive as a threat. Think of a lion about to leap. If you get scared and ready to flee or stay and take it on, you were ready. Today, scientists call it a fight or flight mentality. What's less talked about (and just as harmful) is the third "f" in that equation: freezing. Just like it sounds, freezing happens when, instead of running or fighting, you freeze up at a conflict, unable to make a move to help get you out of that situation.[1]

Make the Move

Has there been a time when you were ready to fight for no real reason?

_____

_____

Using the survival scale rate your response: _____

73

What is one thing you could have done to move up one degree? How would that have helped you? _____

_____

_____

How about run away from a positive opportunity or situation simply because you felt uncomfortable?

_____

_____

Using the survival scale rate your response: _____

What is one thing you could have done to move up one degree? How would that have helped you? _____

_____

_____

Have you ever felt frozen?

_____

_____

_____

Using the survival scale rate your response:

_____

What is one thing you could have done to move up one degree? How would that have helped you? _____

_____

_____

These fight, flight, and freeze responses no longer serve us in this delayed-results environment, and we need to do the work to make sure our bodies and minds have caught up. Does a test being stressful warrant you running away from it? Do you really need to fight someone who supposedly "disrespected" you to preserve your next meal? The emotions that once kept us alive now lead us to death, incarceration, and under employment (or even unemployment) in our day-to-day lives.

You can see people who put emotions first shut down quickly: think of how poorly some people respond to feedback. Even if someone points out three things they do well and offers one place that needs improvement, many people are inclined to only hear the bad. The next time you get feedback, try something different: take it as a genuine step on your ladder of self-growth. Setting aside emotions can be tough at first, but to make it, you'll need to look at the big picture using reason, not reaction.

Our ancestors lived in the moment, unable to plan for the far future while under constant threat of animal attacks or natural disasters, and so we evolved to put our emotions first. Because our society is consumed by power, privilege, and injustice, many people find themselves forced to scramble for their basic needs and think the immediate-results mentality is the best way to survive. After all, you gotta eat to survive— just not in a way that kills you. The U.S. is the junk food capital of the world, and getting fed that way doesn't push you toward that six. Since when has using destructive actions to meet basic needs become survival?

Looking back at Maslow's Hierarchy of Needs (see 1.6), we can better understand this dangerous paradox. Working from the bottom (the most basic needs) all the way to the top, the pyramid goes like this:

1. **Physiological needs**
   These are your basics of basics, like food, water, and shelter

2. **Safety**
   This can be emotional, financial, mental, or physical, but it comes down to feeling safe and at ease in all immediate facets of your life

3. **Social belonging**
   This is where you fit in with your friends, family, and communities

4. **Esteem**
   When you have your basic needs met, you can better focus on learning to love and respect yourself.

5. **Self-Actualization**
   This is similar to the fifth step of change (see 1.8), when you've acquired goals you set for yourself. Maybe you have a dream job, home, or romantic situation.

6. **Transcendence**
   This is a more recent addition to the pyramid. Once you've achieved your goals, the final place is in giving back—maybe making an impact in the community or by getting involved in spiritual practices.

Maslow argued that actions develop to meet your needs, but what many people don't want to acknowledge is the role that power, privilege, and injustice plays (see 1.4) in making it so much harder for some people to meet those needs. When you couple that dynamic with thousands of years of evolutionary automatic reactions, it's easy to see why so many people resort to that do-or-die stance. But what sense does it make to meet a need if meeting that need contributes to your death, incarceration, or long-term demise?

To get out of a situation of scarcity, you need forward planning, some risk-taking (at least in terms of investing money in new skills) and a willingness to do work for the long haul. Although you may have acted in your immediate, fear-based way with possibly misunderstood intentions for your wellbeing, methodical and forward thinking is your only way to survive in this modern landscape.[2]

The real question to ask yourself is this: which of your emotions serve your survival in a delayed-return environment?

Make the Move

What are three things you've done when acting out of anger or fear that came from an immediate-return mindset?	On a scale of one to six, how did it help your true survival?
1.	
2.	
3.	

Look at those three actions above and visualize the situations that caused them. What are three things you could have done instead in those moments?

Make the Move

What could you have done instead to push you toward the six?	What can you do to help you be ready to respond this way next time?
1.	
2.	
3.	

When it comes to emotional development, it helps to be aware of the context in which your social and emotional status have evolved. Successful young people understand the reasons behind emotions; with the right support and tools, these emotions can be managed healthily.

We're not living like our ancestors did, and if you want to make it, your job now is to adapt: face those things that are difficult or even terrifying. Your brain may scream in protest at first, trying to keep you from doing the things that it believes could hurt you, but if you're going to seek out a delayed-results mentality, you have to let go of that panic and trust yourself to see things through.

The situations that trigger our emotions are often unreal, but don't beat yourself up. Instead, take control. If you can change the way you see or interpret a situation, you can change the emotion behind it.

Our perceptions are wrong more often than you'd think.[3] You may feel like someone doesn't like you when in reality they don't even have an opinion about you! You may think that a company would never hire you based on a record or qualifications when really the hiring manager was once like you and more willing to take a chance on you than you'd thought. What if, instead of walking around with the idea that nobody cares or wants to help, you moved through the world believing that others can care and that relationships you build can lead you to true survival?

Negative emotions can be traced back to two provoking points: physical or social safety. Anything you perceive—whether correctly or incorrectly—as a physical or social threat will elicit an emotional response. It's on you to navigate that. But don't worry, we'll help you get there.

3.2. Social Emotional Learning

There are studies linking the importance of what researchers coined "socio-emotional learning" to your MAKiN iT journey.[4] Socio-emotional learning can be described as the way that people acquire and use the knowledge, attitudes, or skills needed for managing emotions, achieving positive goals, feeling and showing empathy, maintaining positive relationships, and making responsible decisions.[5]

Put plainly, that means successful young adults are always working to absorb information before going off on some automatic rampage. How do they do it? By consistently putting in the effort to work on and build the five key socioemotional learning skills and abilities:

1. **Self-Awareness**
    This is how well you can look at your emotions and values and see how they impact your behavior. By analyzing yourself honestly, you can begin to let go of the flawed logic that may have you in its grips. Having good self-awareness puts you in a growth mindset instead of in a fixed mindset that doesn't let you absorb new information.

2. **Social Awareness**
    This is how well you can put yourself in someone else's shoes. This empathy goes a long way in making sure you act in ways that have your true survival in mind. With social awareness, you are also keyed into what the standards are for MAKiN iT in your community, neighborhood, or city, and can appreciate different viewpoints, backgrounds, and lifestyles.

3. **Self-Management**
    Self-management is a key element to your social-emotional learning. With your awareness in mind, self-management helps you keep emotions in check, manage stress, and communicate your needs calmly and clearly. This is the difference between causing fistfights that can land you in jail or walking away with a clear head.

4. **Decision-making Skills**

   To make it, you have to be able to clearly identify the real problems and dangers in your life and learn how to keep those dangers at bay. By figuring out what really points you to true survival, you'll be confident you're maximizing your time and making decisions that push you to your six.

5. **Relationship Skills**

   Finally, building and keeping up healthy, rewarding relationships with diverse people is critical to success. Through making a variety of friends, you learn how to communicate better, listen well, cooperate with folks who are different from you, bounce back from negative peer pressure, and seek or give help when needed.[6]

In chapter one, we talked about the immediate-results mindset and its impact on our actions, tools, values, and beliefs and how that impacted our success. Whether we push towards the six or the one often comes down to our emotional energy at the given moment. When we're content, our actions tend to be positive and success-affirming, but when we're overcome with anger or sadness, our actions can veer off into destructive territory.

Very rarely do gang members get up in the morning, eat some Rice Krispies, kiss their grandmas, and then head on out to do dirt and violence. More often, their actions are preceded by engaging with the tools, attitudes, beliefs, and behaviors that prep them for the do-dirt mental state. Drug use, violent language, hype, and misdirection are all key ingredients of what it takes to harm someone. Have you ever seen a fight break out where people are yelling positive or encouraging things at each other? Didn't think so. The bottom line is that to do dark, you must go dark. It's the same with light: to get in that light, first you've got to shine.

3.3. The Infinite Drama

People throw away their life, freedom, or future economic opportunity over something as stupid as being called a name. Why do we let a so-called disrespect get the better of us and lead us to our demise?

M̲ Make the Move M̲

What are the top five ways you've seen negative emotions destroy someone's life, freedom, or FEO?
1.
2.
3.
4.
5.

We call those emotional situations that drag you to the one the infinite drama. Successful young people know that the only way to truly stop the infinite drama is to never let it start from the get-go. It's hard, but over time, you can do it. Some things will always be beyond your control: where you were born, who your parents are, what horrible experiences occurred in your childhood. What is within your control is every step you take moving forward. If you're sick and tired of the infinite drama, remember: it isn't your fault. You were born into it. What's on you though, are the steps you take here on out. There's a way up; just keep reading.

Feelings of disrespect can cause people to kick their life, freedom, and FEO to the curb. In the long term, it doesn't make sense, yet so many people lose control and hurt another person for simply feeling disrespected. People wind up in jail over road rage, being called names, or even just getting bumped into while in the line at McDonald's. Overreacting always costs a higher price than what you get in return. Keep the future in your pocket and letting go of other people's anger will come more and more easily.

3.4. Tales from the Bright Side

Ray and Rory used to be like two peas in a pod, tighter than Redman and Method Man. Homeboys to the end, they said. They worked as lookouts for a dealer in their neighborhood. When a local youth worker got wind of what they were up to, he invited them to the youth center to explore other options for making money. Intrigued, Ray and Rory took him up on his invitation. After a little talking and some free pizza, they told the youth worker they worked for the dealer to buy new clothes and sneakers and for a little spending money in their pockets.

The youth worker smiled and encouraged them to find legitimate employment. Ray nodded, and Rory followed after a second. They all three agreed that if the boys could find a job that would earn them each $125 a week, they would leave the drug business for good. The youth worker said it would take three weeks to prepare for the job search, including learning how to fill out a job application, how to master some techniques for nailing an interview, and how to hold down a job once you got it. Once they'd done that, the youth worker continued, they would go apply. If they couldn't find a job in a month, the youth worker said he'd give them one at the local center.

On the way out, the youth worker shook both their hands. Ray was excited, but as the door closed behind them, Rory sneered and told Ray he wouldn't be going back. He had thought the youth worker was making fun of them by offering them this chance. "I won't be caught dead doing something embarrassing like bagging groceries, man." Ray shook his head.

Over the next few weeks, Ray came back, and Rory didn't. Within a month, Ray got a job. Eventually, he completed high school, then enrolled in community college. Rory kept to the dealing circuit and recently got shot after a fight and died.

Rory thought he was disrespected, but Ray saw the youth worker's offer as an opportunity to make it. Who will you be?

code: Infinite drama...the only way to stop it is to never start it.

Make the Move

What are ten ways people say they can be disrespected?	How can they handle it in a way that leads them to the six?
1.	
2.	
3.	
4.	
5.	
6.	
7.	
8.	
9.	
10.	

3.5. Trauma

Some young people are lucky enough to enjoy a drama-free childhood. For others, maybe like yourself, growing up left you haunted by traumatic events, abuse, and hardship.

The statistics in our country paint a bleak picture:

- 60% of all children experience or are exposed to abuse of some kind
- 3.3 million children witness domestic violence each year[7]
- 34% of LGBT youth have been bullied or threatened at school[8]
- 40% of children are said to experience physical assault while 10% are injured[9]
- One in three girls under eighteen will experience sexual assault or violence[10]
- 25% of kids are victims of theft or vandalism[11]
- 14% report being treated badly by caregivers while 4% experience physical abuse[12]
- 13% of children are reportedly bullied while 33% say they were emotionally bullied[13]
- 20% witness violence in their neighborhood or at home[14]

These statistics impact are more than just a number: youth who experience trauma are fifteen times more likely to commit suicide and four times more likely to use substances, drink, or contract STDs, and these traumatic events also increase the likelihood of depression, diseases, financial struggles, stress, and anger problems.[15]

In 2012, a study suggested that childhood stress can have a dramatic effect on our DNA. It proposed that emotional trauma brought on by bullying or exposure to violence or domestic abuse can shorten parts of our DNA called telomeres, which are found at the ends of our chromosomes. These telomeres keep DNA from unraveling but can lead to biological aging and health problems when shortened.[16]

Emotions can also impact your brain development. While developing, teens tend to lean on their amygdalas—a region of the brain linked to emotions and impulsive behavior – to make decisions, rather than the prefrontal cortex, or rational part of your brain.[17]

That is because the prefrontal cortex doesn't fully develop until the age of twenty-five. Even though the brain reaches 90-95% of its adult size by age six, a pruning process takes place during the teen years that removes unused connections. Because the brain is so malleable (capable of being molded) at this stage of growth, you need to ensure that you can positively hone your rationalizing and feeling skills.[18]

However, just as trauma can negatively impact our brain and our DNA, we have the power to push it in the opposite direction toward learning, growth, and intelligence. This concept is known as the growth mindset. Coined by Dr. Carol S. Dweck, the growth mindset is based on the idea that if you believe you can improve yourself and put in the appropriate effort, time, and strategies, you will get smarter. This includes developing your emotional intelligence, too.[19]

But teenagers don't have it easy: most older people don't know how to help young adults deal with emotions. They are unaware of the trauma you have gone through and may ask unintentionally rude questions like, "What's wrong with you?" instead of "What happened that made you react that way? How can we work together to resolve it?"

Teachers are trained to teach students and to convey information, but they're not necessarily equipped to address trauma. Instead, seek out people trained to talk about it. Youth health clinics are safe places to find professionals who can help you and ask the right questions.

The various kinds of professional help out there can feel overwhelming, but there are two specific forms of treatment that address the many faces of trauma:

Trauma-informed care (TIC) is a treatment approach that recognizes clients can experience many types of trauma, including drug use, domestic violence, and child abuse. TIC emphasizes safety (emotional, physical, and psychological), trust, choice, collaboration, and empowering the individual. Clients can be easily re-traumatized during other treatment methods, so TIC focuses on full support and understanding for deep healing.

Motivational interviewing is a form of counseling that deals with a client's feelings and insecurities to help them resolve issues. Like TIC, empowerment is the core of this practice. Motivational interviewing acknowledges how hard it is to make changes in life and employs a thoughtful and practical approach. Typically, motivational interviewing is used for addiction and anger management.

Like millions of young adults, you may have encountered situations that stirred up negative emotions. Fortunately, you have the power to cultivate techniques for coping with them.

Lisa M. Schab, a Chicago-based social worker and author, wrote a book called *The Self-Esteem Workbook for Teens: Activities to Help You Build Confidence and Achieve Your Goals*. In it, she argues that "managing feelings is one of the most important skills we ever learn." To help young people manage their emotions, she recommends four simple steps:

1. Name the feeling. What is the emotion you're experiencing?
2. Accept what you're feeling. Instead of avoiding it, embrace it. If you hide it, it can instead intensify and explode. Try saying to yourself, "It's OK to feel [insert emotion]."
3. Express your feelings. Talk to someone you trust, write them down, cry, or exercise to help release some of the energy bubbling in you. Just don't hurt yourself or others.
4. Engage in some self-care. Think of something positive and comforting for you. It could be going for a walk, napping, getting a hug, taking a shower, drinking coffee with a friend, or anything nourishing and helpful for processing your negative emotions.[20]

If you aren't vibing with this process, no worries. There are still plenty of ways to avoid infinite drama. Read over these techniques and find one you can roll with:

- **Meditation**
  Meditation helps to calm the mind. Find a quiet space where you can comfortably sit in a relaxed position. Close your eyes and concentrate on your breathing. Inhale and exhale slowly. If thoughts or sounds distract you, it's okay. Return to your breathing. Do this for about ten minutes, if possible. (There are many free sitting groups in different cities, or check YouTube for guided meditations to help you get started.)

- **Progressive Muscle Relaxation (PMR)**
  This is a process where you tense different muscle groups for five seconds, then relax them slowly for thirty seconds. Start at your toes and work up your body. PMR helps you relax and become aware of how your body physically reacts to stress.

- **Write down an emotion and throw it away.**
  By writing your thoughts down on paper, crumpling it up, and shooting it into the trash like a basketball, you can help release your negative emotions. This helps you take control of what you're feeling.

- **Self-Soothing**
  This technique helps you refocus your energy away from negative emotions. Find a comfortable spot, focus on breathing, then isolate your five senses (hearing, smell, sight, taste, and touch). Spend a minute concentrating on each. What sounds do you hear? What do you smell? What details can you see around you? Do you taste anything? What can you feel under your hands, feet, or legs?

- **Journaling**
  It can be hard to clearly express your emotions. By writing down your thoughts, you can find clarity or just work out how you're feeling. Don't stress about the format of what you're writing. By getting it out on paper over time, you can process your emotions and stumble across solutions.

- **Positive Visualization**
  Replace negative thoughts or feelings with images that invoke positive feelings. This can be a memory, someone who inspires you, or visualizations of future, positive plans. Go back to your five senses. The more details you can visualize, the better!

If these suggestions don't help, reach out to a therapist or counselor. If you are feeling suicidal, call the National Suicide Prevention Lifeline at 1-800-273-8255. They offer free and confidential support twenty-four hours a day, seven days a week. Remember, there's always a way forward to a brighter future.

Unchecked emotions can lead to violence, death, and getting locked up. In our country, homes, and local communities, we witness so much violence that we've grown numb. It's time to wake up, stand up, and act against violence. The easiest place to start is with yourself.

Violence breeds anger, which is just another emotion that inhibits your success. Anger in the workplace can be disastrous. What if someone says something rude and you're not in control of your emotions? You're likely to go off and lose your job. Anger and success just don't mix.

Anger has never served your journey toward the six. Why keep repeating the same missteps and hoping that this time they'll lead you to success?

Make the Move

What's a way someone can disrespect you?	What emotions come up from it?	What actions do you take based on those emotions?	What are the ultimate consequences for you and the person involved?

If you translate disrespect as a negative emotion, it will surely have a negative result, so how do we make it a positive outcome? Check this out. The next time you feel like someone has disrespected you, take it as a lesson learned. If someone plays you, say, "Okay, good thing I know the real deal," or "Thank God I saw their true side." Remember conditioning (see 1.5). It only seems hard to change this because you've been trained to react a certain way. But if you keep doing the same thing and turning up with the same results, maybe it's time to try something different.

Certain decisions go a long way to promote our life, freedom, and FEO. Others work against them. All you have to do is think over each decision. Do you want to stay alive and free? Do you want to make that paper—or do you want to get locked up or never land a decent job?

3.6. Work Through It

You may be nervous about trying to work in a big company because you feel like you're not "professional" enough. Remember, that's only a perception. Once you start working, you'll quickly learn what professional standards your job holds. Then you'll have a real bar to work toward. That might mean something as easy as swapping out that tank-top for a button-down (or your halter top for a blouse) and holding back on the slang a bit.

Maybe you've heard about how hard it is to interview, and just thinking about sitting across from an older adult and getting blasted with questions has you breaking out in a nervous sweat. *What if she asks me about why I didn't graduate in the top of my class? What if he asks about why I left school? What if they ask about my child?* Remember that a fear of these questions is based on perceptions, not reality.

If an interviewer has decided to meet with you, they're genuinely considering hiring you and are using the interview to find reasons to do so. This interview is your time to give them those reasons. Always go into an interview believing you have a lot to offer an employer. If you left school for personal problems, be up front. Let them know you're a different person now and are looking for opportunities to grow. Most interviewers agree that the best way to get through an interview is by staying relaxed and speaking honestly.

By acknowledging fears and dealing with them head-on, you will be pleasantly surprised by how much easier things are than your mind has made them out to be. Work through it, one emotion at a time, and you'll find success not far around the corner.

3.7. Tales from the Bright Side

Rocky's pain was so intense that it was hard to appreciate anyone, even those who'd tried to help him. Rocky's mother abandoned the family when he was eight, and his father, who was always drunk and hardly seemed to notice Rocky was around, raised him. If it hadn't been for his grandmother, Rocky never would have made it.

Rocky leaned on his chosen family: his homeboys in the streets were his life. They did everything together, including getting into trouble and dropping out. As it tends to, that trouble reached a head one day, and Rocky was sentenced to nine months in prison. When he finally got out, the courts ordered him to go into a job-training program where he met Cliff, who was both a counselor and an ex-con. Cliff and Rocky had had similar upbringings, so he knew where Rocky was coming from—and wasn't afraid to get in his face about doing the right thing. Some of the other counselors were turned off by Rocky's prickly attitude, but not Cliff. He knew that what Rocky needed was for someone to challenge his actions and beliefs. By talking about their fathers, the pain of prison, and the seduction of money, Cliff helped Rocky reckon with the anger that consumed him. By working through it with Cliff, his friend and mentor, Rocky found the confidence to become a carpenter apprentice, where he's been earning $17 an hour for the past year.

Like Rocky, the road ahead becomes smoother once you learn how to manage conflict without resorting to violence. You have to learn the skills that will enable you to avoid outside pressures to get wrapped up in violence. Many young adults get violent because a group pressures them into it. Don't be one of those people—think for yourself. Remember, you're in control if you develop the courage and ability to leave potentially violent situations.

Developing something called emotional intelligence or emotional quotient (EQ) can give you the upper hand when dealing with potential employers. Your EQ is the ability to identify and manage your emotions and recognize others' emotions. Demonstrating a high EQ shows that you can handle what life throws at you, manage stress and feedback, and have empathy for coworkers and customers. Increasing it not only helps your job search but can significantly improve your personal relationships. EQ is just as important as IQ in the workplace, if not more so.

Successful young adults who were scared about interviewing have told us that once the interview began, they calmed down. If you let your fears hold you back from going to an interview, you'll never gain anything. You've got to be able to put those negative thoughts in check. Let's see what some young adults had to say about their emotions and interviewing.

"I felt very tense. I was nervous and sweaty all over. It was tough, but I knew what I was doing. Actually, you can control the questions that are given to you; it depends on how you answer them. If you give short responses that are legitimate and simple, you can get out of the really tough questions quickly."

"At first I was nervous. It was something I'd never done before, so I was wondering how I would excel in that position. But I was enthusiastic and had prepared ahead of time, so I got through it. They ended up hiring me, so I would say it went very well."

"I had an answer ready for every question; that made things much easier."

"The first three times I was nervous because they were my first times going on interviews. But by the last two, I calmed down a great deal. I started to see it was easy, so it got easy on me."

Make the Move

List the emotions that you believe are keeping you from making it.

_____

_____

_____

_____

What caused you to develop these emotions?

_____

_____

_____

_____

_____

For each emotion listed above, how would you like to feel?

_____

What steps or actions would you need to take to control some of these emotions?

_____

MAKiN iT is a journey, and every journey must have a purpose. Imagine going on a trip without knowing where you're going or why you're trying to get there. Why do you want to make it? What is it you want to achieve? To be a success, you need to know the answer to these questions. Imagine: if Dr. Martin Luther King, Jr. hadn't had a purpose, he might have given up when the going got rough.

On your own path, you'll face difficulties—some real, some imagined. What supports this journey is finding that "why" like Malik did at the beginning of the chapter. Simon Sinek, motivational speaker and author of *Find Your Why*, puts it best: "Achievement happens when we pursue and attain what we want. Success comes when we are in clear pursuit of why we want it."

This "why" infuses meaning into everything you do, allowing you to sacrifice things in the present with an eye to your gains in the future. Knowing that there's a reason for your actions gives you the strength and confidence to succeed.

Your purpose is *not* your job. Your purpose is the reason for being here and a statement about what you're looking to accomplish. "I'm a lawyer" is not a purpose statement. "I want to help empower other people and end the school-to-prison pipeline" is. Purpose statements are powerful tools, letting you and others know why you're here. If you choose to live life by a purpose, you're taking charge of your life in a way that most young adults can never imagine. Your purpose evolves as you get older and become more aware of the needs of the world, your community, and—

most importantly—yourself, but the first step to that ultimate purpose is forming the foundations of one now.

A statement of your purpose, vision, or "why" helps you connect with older adults as well. To help you get going, try writing a YOUTRY statement. This statement is part of anchoring, or the process of getting someone emotionally invested in helping you achieve those FEO goals. This YOUTRY statement is a clear, memorable script that you can reference whenever you get the opportunity to connect with an adult.

To be effective, a YOUTRY statement checks these five boxes:

1. You introduce yourself to the potential connect

2. You identify your goals and aspirations.

3. You define why you want to attain these goals.

4. You ask for help in achieving them.

5. You collect the connection's contact information to follow up.

With a YOUTRY statement in your pocket, you can confidently approach any potential connection. Adults are always looking for ways to help young people who are helping themselves, and your readiness won't go unnoticed.

Interested in checking out more about the YOUTRY statement and other social-capital-building skills? Check out *Making Connections Work* by Edward DeJesus, which can be found on the Social Capital Builders website (www.socialcapitalbuilders.com) and on Amazon.

Let's take the time to develop your own purpose statement.

▨ **Make the Move** ▨

Where do I want my life to go?

_____

_____

_____

Why do I want to get there?

- -

- -

- -

Take a look at your various roles in life. In each role, you have a position you play. What is it? Take time to think about your different roles. We have some listed below, as well as blank spaces for you to add any other roles that apply to you. Next to these roles, write down two words you want people to say about how you perform in that position.

When you have named your roles and positions, put it all together and create an ownership statement. Write an "I am" statement for each role to put how you said you want people to see you into the present moment.

Example: Employee: 1. Hard working, 2. Dedicated
Ownership statement: I am a hardworking employee who is dedicated to my job.

Son/Daughter: _____

   Ownership statement: _____

Parent: _____

   Ownership statement: _____

Friend: _____

   Ownership statement: _____

Student: _____

   Ownership statement: _____

Employee: _____

   Ownership statement: _____

Athlete: _____

   Ownership statement: _____

Artist: _____

   Ownership statement: _____

Sibling: _____

   Ownership statement: _____

   Ownership statement: _____

   Ownership statement: _____

Put all these ownership statements together and you'll have your purpose statement. If everything you do doesn't relate back to this statement, then you're just wasting time. The best purpose statement always takes a few attempts to write well—don't stress about it. At the end, you should have a clear and concise statement to serve as the reason for your success journey.

My Purpose Statement:

_____

_____

_____

_____

Take some time over the next few weeks to refine the paragraph above, really making sure you're clear on what it means. Tape your statement to your mirror or any place where you'll see it daily. Ask yourself: are my actions in line with my purpose? If the answer is yes, you're heading in the right direction. If the answer is no, realign your actions with your purpose ASAP. The direction you take is in your hands, and your purpose is your compass. Now it's on you to take the next steps.

I got way too much on my mental, I learn from what I've been through. I'm finna do what I didn't do – and still waking up like the rent's due.

- Drake

UNIVERSAL SUCCESS HABIT FOUR:

Successful Young Adults Consistently Inventory and Improve Their Skills and Habits

DeMarcus bent over, hands against his thighs, as he tried to catch his breath. He'd never run that fast before—hadn't even thought he could. His brother Tyson's sneakers slapped against the alley pavement as he stopped by DeMarcus, leaning against a wall. It only took a minute before cops rounded the corner, guns held out. DeMarcus stepped in front of his brother, his hands up.

Glancing back at Tyson, he grimaced. "Sorry, man."

Breaking and entering had seemed like a good idea at the time. Their grandma did her best to take care of them, but most of the time there just wasn't enough food in the house—breakfast and lunch were hard to come by, especially with school out for the summer. When DeMarcus saw his little brother's face twist with hunger pangs that morning, he took the situation into his own hands.

They walked through Newport News, scouting a place to get some food. It took two hours of shuffling through neighborhoods, but finally, a house stood gleaming and empty. They sneaked over to the backyard gate and unlatched it, finding the sliding glass door unlocked like the *place was made for them. Hesitating for only a second in the doorframe, Tyson ran to the fridge, his eyes widening when he opened it. How could one family have so much food in the fridge? He stared, slack-jawed, before shaking his head and getting out the sliced turkey and tomatoes.*

Tyson and DeMarcus ate over the sink, licking the crumbs off their fingers when DeMarcus glanced up to see a patrol car rolling up to the front of the house. Grabbing his brother's arm, they made a mad dash out the back, ending in the alley, out of breath and out of options.

"I swear on my momma's grave, we just ran into that house to make some food!" As the cops swooped up with handcuffs, DeMarcus glanced at his baby brother again, shame flooding his cheeks. This wasn't how getting Tyson fed was supposed to go down.

Caught red-handed, the brothers were sent up to Bon Air Juvenile Correctional Center, which was over an hour's drive from their hometown. Visitation was allowed, but since their grandma didn't have a ride, the boys rarely saw her.

Twelve months passed—months when DeMarcus would have finished high school and during which Tyson shot up like a reed. When they got back home, their grandma held them both, the wrinkles in the corners of her eyes damp. She took a step back, her jaw set.

"If I catch you two getting into any type of trouble again, you're out. You hear me?"

"Yes ma'am," they replied in unison.

DeMarcus looked at his grandma, pushing sixty, yet able to bring the fear of God into anyone who crossed her or her family. Ever since their parents had died in a crash a few years back, she had looked after DeMarcus and Tyson like a mama bear. She loved having them in the home, but having her grandbabies meant more mouths to feed; she was rarely around, picking up shifts at the store to make ends meet. The night they came back, she watched the streetlights through the blinds, praying DeMarcus and Tyson would stay out of trouble. Virginia had one of the highest recidivism rates in the U.S., and she knew it. Out of the youth who served at Bon Air, 74% were arrested again in three years—Bon Air didn't exactly prep their inmates for a bright future once they got out. She rolled over in bed, pushing the thoughts from her mind, and tried to find sleep.

Their first Saturday out, DeMarcus and Tyson went to the park. They came across a group of ten people huddled in a cipher. The boys were both nice with rhymes; DeMarcus often wrote them on his own time, jotting down ideas to vibe off other people. The group widened to allow them in the circle. As he stepped in, DeMarcus locked eyes with the guy he'd been hoping to avoid: Malcolm. He glanced away, determined to exchanging bars and enjoy the moment.

Malcolm clapped DeMarcus and Tyson each on the back. "Yo, it's good to see ya both out."

DeMarcus leaned back, seeing Tyson beam at him. Malcolm was known for trappin on the block. He'd always wanted the brothers to get involved but hadn't been able to sell them on the idea before, but seeing them fresh out of Bon Air, he tried again. "You back at grandma's? If you need anything, I gotchu, fam."

DeMarcus always viewed Malcolm as sus. Drug-pushing aside, he came off extra, and DeMarcus didn't trust him. Still, he smiled before he replied, "Nah, me and Tyson good."

That night, DeMarcus was still ramped up after the cipher that morning and found an old spiral-bound notebook from his high school days. Rifling through it, he got to an empty page and started reflecting on his time in Bon Air. Writing cleared his head—and made him tired. His eyes sagged as he laid in bed with the notebook, and he slept so deeply he didn't hear Tyson sneak out of the house to see what Malcolm had to offer.

His grandma shouting shook DeMarcus awake. Tyson was gone. Muttering under his breath, DeMarcus threw on his clothes and went into the streets to scoop up Tyson.

He found Malcolm first. "Yo, where's Tyson?"

As soon as he saw Malcolm's smirk, DeMarcus knew he was involved with his brother's disappearance. "Don't worry. I've got him working now—at least somebody in your family will be earning."

DeMarcus shoved Malcolm and took off looking for Tyson again.

After an hour of searching turned him up empty-handed, DeMarcus went home to break the news to his grandma to find Tyson sitting on the couch. His grandma's face was a mask. "He told me he's working for Malcolm now." She glanced over at Tyson, her trembling voice determined. "I told you you'd be out of here if you got yourself mixed up in something."

Tyson shoved off the couch, avoiding DeMarcus's eye as he went into their shared bedroom and started stuffing his things into a duffel bag. "I'm done with having nothin'!" he yelled out to them. "I gotta get my paper up."

His shoulder brushed DeMarcus' as he walked out the door. DeMarcus called his brother's name, but the door slamming was his only reply. In less than three months, Tyson caught a case—this time, he was facing years in prison.

In the weeks after he heard about Tyson's arrest, DeMarcus blamed himself. He should have never gone into that house to get food, should have made sure Tyson never linked up with Malcolm. The anger and frustration seemed like it would suffocate him; he decided to pay Malcolm a visit, but first, he had to get a gun. Getting a piece was easy, and it only took DeMarcus an hour before he got his hands on a .38 snub-nose revolver from a hookup down the block. Head down, he headed to the corner, peeping Malcolm at his usual spot. The metal in his pocket was so cold he thought it would burn his hand, but before he could pull it from his jacket pocket, an old friend came out of the corner store with a bag of groceries.

"What's good, DeMarcus? It's been a minute!" Rasheed's smile stretched across his face, and DeMarcus found himself smiling back despite himself. Rasheed was a few years older, and DeMarcus hadn't seen him since he'd made it out of the hood, but as kids, they'd been inseparable.

DeMarcus let go of the gun in his pocket like a man shaken from a trance—what he'd been about to do was crazy, and he knew it. "Yo, Rasheed. How ya been?"

"You got time? Let me buy you a coffee and hear about your life!" DeMarcus glanced at Malcolm, oblivious on the corner, and took

Rasheed up on the offer. They walked a few blocks to a coffee shop, and DeMarcus told him all about what happened with him and Tyson. They caught up at the shop for hours; it felt good to get these struggles off his chest. Just like when they were kids, Rasheed was a good listener, and he had done well for himself in the years since. He'd gotten accepted to the University of Virginia, he said. DeMarcus nodded, impressed. Rasheed had gotten into his fair share of trouble but straightened up in high school. Best of all, even though Rasheed wasn't in the hood anymore, he was still easy to relate to.

"How'd you do it, man?"

"I remember the day like it was yesterday. I'd gotten into a fight with a kid over some petty shit and the cops rolled up. We started talking back to them. They roughed us up good, kicking us and slamming me against the hood of the car like I'd just shot someone. Broke three ribs. Sitting in that jail cell, I knew I had to change."

"So, what did you do?"

"I made a choice. Changed my behavior. Instead of being on the block all day, I started doing my homework. When my homework was done, I picked up any book I could get my hands on. Reading more, it made me shift my attitude too, and I started treating others with respect regardless of whether I liked them or not. And once I got a book on fitness, I started working out and eating healthier. Before I knew it, all that healthy living had my head clear enough to focus on bigger goals, like getting into college."

DeMarcus fiddled with his coffee cup. "Look at me, man. I got no job. No education. How's someone like me supposed to change?" His voice was low, and he avoided Rasheed's eye.

"You gotta start by looking at—really looking at—all your strengths and weaknesses, then build from there. Ignore all the noise on the block—none of it will save you. You have to do that for yourself."

After they'd finished their coffees, Rasheed put DeMarcus' number in his phone and shot him a text with his number. "Text me if you ever need something, okay? I got you."

The whole time at the coffee shop, the revolver had been like a weight in his pocket, and he got rid of it as quickly as he could. He was done chasing that life. Later that week, he called up Rasheed. He sounded genuinely happy to hear from DeMarcus and offered to help him change his life up.

Within two months, DeMarcus was a new person. He woke up early, ate fruit instead of sugar-filled cereal, exercised, and read a book a week. Rasheed had shown him how to embrace a growth mindset and build better habits through something called habit stacking and the 2/1/30 rule: two new skills and one new habit every thirty days. Starting with small goals, DeMarcus moved himself up the ladder. In just sixty days, he'd read eight books, learned some conversational Spanish, and gotten into the best shape of his life.

Rasheed had been right—living healthier cleared his head. DeMarcus realized he should get a job using the thing he'd always enjoyed: writing. By renting books from the library and taking a free introductory class online, he sharpened his skills. With Rasheed's help, he applied to an entry-level copyediting job and even learned how to tie a tie so he'd look professional at the interview. The hiring manager was impressed by DeMarcus' focus and took a chance on him.

By building new habits and skills, DeMarcus didn't need to become a statistic like his brother; he had a future to look forward to.

4.1. You got this!

Many young adults know how to dribble a basketball but can't tie a tie. They can spit rhymes from three years ago but can't begin to answer ten basic interview questions. Each year at the MAKiN iT seminars, we offer $20 to a participant who can do one of three things successfully:

1. Answer the question "tell me about yourself" within a minute—and without saying "um," "uh," or "ah."
2. Write a fifty-word response to an opening for an entry-level job.
3. Tie a tie.

Although we've done over five thousand presentations, we can count on two hands the number of times we've given that $20 up to someone. Now is there something wrong with dribbling a basketball or rhyming? Of course not. But there's something wrong with not working on the skills that promote your future economic opportunity on top of your pastimes. It goes back to that immediate-results mentality again. Unless your name is Drake or Steph Curry (and if you're reading this, I'm guessing it's not), rhyming and ballin' have little to do with earning money. This book is about true survival and success, and that means keeping it one hundred with you. We're not playing games—we're showing you how to make it.

Success can be easy if you have caring adults, a supportive peer group, and genuine, culturally competent opportunities to work and learn, but it's hard to get ahold of that key and use it when you're trapped in the immediate-results mentality. Don't let the media dupe you into thinking that a pair of sneakers and wild attitude will make you successful. In Thomas Staley's book *The Millionaire Next Door*, he reveals a secret truth about the wealthy: most millionaires drive a ten-year-old car, live in the same house the always lived in, and still have a job.[1]

Living only for immediate results makes you focus on habits and skills that don't lead you to long-term success, and they can actually lead to your demise. That immediate-results mindset makes doing homework, going to a program to learn a skill, or reading up on interview questions look like a waste of time. But how do you think others before you have developed those skills? A delayed-results mindset gives you the motivation you need to develop those skills and habits. When you have your eye on that long-term prize—your life, freedom, and FEO—then doing the things that seem less fun to you now will yield some serious results down the line.

No matter how corny it sounds, remember: you are the future. Growing up is hard enough on its own, but throw in misrepresenters and that immediate-results environment, and the path is overrun with obstacles. Youth are faced with oppressive issues on the daily. Discrimination, homophobia, racism, sexism, you name it—young people everywhere are dealing with issues they feel can't be fixed. Despite all of that, you have the power to make it as long as you take ownership in developing the skills that propel you to the six and seek out people who can help.

How do you make that first move? Like DeMarcus, it starts with improving those skills and habits, and the best way to accomplish this is by following the 2/1/30 rule: two new skills and one new habit every thirty days. If you keep up with this rule for a year, you'll have twenty-four new skills and twelve new behaviors on lock.

Before you write the idea off as daunting, think about what you can learn in thirty days if you put your heart into it: how to speak in public, the fundamentals of a new language, how to fly a plane. However, you have to have the resources available to make it happen, and this chapter will set the groundwork for you to develop that 2/1/30 by showing you how to be consistent and focused as well as give you some suggestions for skills to start working on.

You may feel frustrated or stressed out by your past and the long road ahead. Just remember, when you learn about delayed-results mentalities on paper and wade back into the everyday, immediate-return life you've been fed, it can be hard to maximize those new skills, and there doesn't seem to be consistent systems in place to help young people figure it out. Just look at the educational system or the workforce system: erasing sixteen to twenty-four years of misrepresentation is just not going to happen in a one-year, underfunded program. Give yourself time to let the changes you're working toward sink in.

When systems are designed for some to fail, it makes social-emotional learning difficult, especially if your home and community culture is different than the culture taught in the classroom. In learning about these skills, educators often look away from how both diversity and broader systems of oppression can keep people from reaching the six in the same way.[2] As you learn about social-emotional learning and as you grow in your own habits, keep in mind that everyone has a different timeline and definition of success, and as long as you're promoting your life, freedom, and FEO, your path might look different from your neighbor's—and that's okay.

4.2.   Skills versus Habits

We've talked a big talk about building two skills and one habit a month, but what's the difference between the two, anyway?

Skills are specific abilities that you do well and in which you have expertise—anything from driving a forklift to playing the piano or writing code. Less talked about (but just as important) are social and emotional skills. While it's possible to learn the skills in theory in a classroom, the real world is where you put them to practice.

Habits, however, are behaviors that you follow and repeat regularly. Some examples are eating well, studying, and exercising regularly. But habits aren't just healthy—there are plenty of destructive ones too, like drinking, abusing substances, and engaging in unprotected sex. All it takes to turn a bad behavior into a destructive habit is repetition. Although they may seem harmless at first, these habits can destroy your whole world. Lucky for you, forming good habits can be just as easy as forming those bad ones.

If you want to develop dope skills and habits, practice is essential.

Ever hear of the Ten-Thousand-Hour Rule? Introduced in Malcolm Gladwell's 2008 best-selling book *Outliers*, the basic concept is that if you want to master something—anything—a huge amount of practice is required: ten thousand hours.[3]

This rule went viral, but not all that publicity was good. According to several experts (including the guy whose research inspired Gladwell to write the book[4]) ten thousand hours won't amount to much if you aren't pushing yourself. People master skills by becoming experts at practicing, an idea known as "deliberate practice." By pushing the boundaries of your capabilities and constantly trying to improve, you can achieve greatness. Think of your favorite athletes, musicians, or actors. They may have been born with height or a strong singing voice, but to be at the top of their game, they had to push themselves—hard.

With deliberate practice, you have to be purposeful and systematic. To make gains, keep your eye on a specific goal. Humans have the tendency to turn behaviors into automatic habits (like going on autopilot). Standard practice is just mindless behavior that reinforces current habits, good or bad. With deliberate practice, we're be mindful of the process, fostering real change.[5]

MAKiN iT isn't about doing one big thing; it's about doing small things with intense focus many, many times, because powerful skills are gained by breaking down the process into manageable steps and testing out new approaches. Good habits are formed by repeating positive behaviors over and over again. With the right mindset and a game plan in hand, you can develop any skill or habit you put your mind to. Believe that, and you'll be unstoppable.

4.3. Make it Happen

In section 3.5, you learned that the brain goes through a kind of pruning process while developing by getting rid of unused connections, but did you know that your brain strengthens the connections you use on the regular, too?

The average adult has 41% fewer neurons than newborns. While that may sound bad, we can strengthen the neural connections we have by learning and forming strong habits. For example, if you practice Spanish every day, you'll build stronger language-learning connections. The more you practice, the faster and stronger you'll get and before you know it, those Spanish skills will be on point.[6]

To bank on this phenomenon and build new skills and habits, consider the two types of mindsets: fixed and growth. People with fixed mindsets are convinced they're stuck with what they got and can't improve, but a growth mindset gives you a better chance of succeeding because you're putting energy into learning, not into what others may think. This focus on improvement is empowering, feeding the growth mindset in a snowball effect for change.

So how do you take on a growth mindset? Here are a few strategies from the experts:

1. **Embrace new ways of learning.**
    We all pick things up differently, so stay curious and experiment with different approaches to find what works best for you.[7]

2. **Develop those mental muscles.**
    Build up your mental toughness and determination instead of leaning on the approval of others. When you get a little mental grit, you can take yourself further than before.[8]

3. **Boost self-awareness.**
    You can't improve yourself if you haven't taken the time to get to really get to know yourself. By understanding who you are and what drives you, you can know what inspires you best.

4. **Ignore the haters.**
   Let go of what others think and open the door to a new world of learning and growth. No matter what you do, there's always going to be at least one hater; don't let them steal your shine.

5. **Reinvent challenges as opportunities.**
   Each roadblock is a chance to learn. Be receptive to that wisdom, embrace difficulties, and you'll come out stronger than ever.[9]

6. **Celebrate growth with others.**
   Like attracts like, and by supporting others in their successes, you can cheer each other on to new heights.

7. **Learn from the mistakes of others.**
   Whether it be a relative, friend, or stranger, everyone screws up. Pay attention to every lesson offered by the people in your life – and learn how to avoid the same pitfalls.[10]

8. **Own your attitude.**
   Your mindset will make or break your progress, and it's the one factor in your life that nobody can shape but you. Keep it positive and reap the benefits.

9. **Be patient.**
   Anything worth having takes time and effort, including new skills and habits.

10. **Focus on the journey, not the destination.**
    It's a learning process. Enjoy the ride, step by step, and find joy in each moment.

We all harbor aspects of fixed and growth mindsets within us; nobody is in either camp entirely. Because we're on this spectrum, everybody deals with fixed-mindset triggers (things that shut down the parts of us that want to grow). These triggers often take the form of challenges, criticism, or setbacks. Identify and deal with these limiting reactions head on. Instead of allowing them to smother your progress, move forward. Prove them wrong. You got this.

4.4. Habit Stacking

Another technique for taking advantage of the pruning process is something called habit stacking. In S.J. Scott's book *Habit Stacking*, he explains how easy it is to grow overwhelmed by making changes in your life. We think we need to take on a bunch of massive goals to improve. Instead, Scott suggests taking on a handful of small habits (think brushing your teeth, making eye contact and smiling, or eating a piece of fruit every day). These, he argues, are the keys to massive improvement.

Take a step back for a second and think of a few things you could do to drastically change your life for the better. What's stopping you? Usually, the answer is too much time or effort. With habit stacking, you develop a group of small habits and make a routine out of it. This way, you can manage your growth with a much more efficient and time-saving approach.

Habit stacking is exactly what it sounds like. Take a current habit like your morning shower, and add a new habit on top of it, like doing twenty jumping jacks before getting in the shower, and you can quickly incorporate the new habit by turning it into a routine. Since the current habit is already hardwired into your daily life, you can effectively link a new habit to that existing, strong network of neural connections, making it much easier to stick with it.[11]

To make sure you're choosing the right habits to stack, follow these eight guidelines:

1. Each habit must take five minutes or less to perform.
2. A habit must be complete without any added effort.
3. All habits must be positive and improve your life.
4. It has to be easy to perform.
5. No routine should take over thirty minutes.
6. Your process needs to be methodical and systematic.
7. Use a checklist to keep yourself on track.
8. The routine should fit your life and ability.[12]

What are some habits you already have? Write them in the table below.

ⓜ Make the Move ⓜ

What are six habits you already have?
1.
2.
3.
4.
5.
6.

In this next table, write down six habits you'd like to have on the left. Some examples are flossing, jumping jacks, eating a piece of fruit, or getting to bed before midnight. On the right, write down which existing habit you can add these six habits to (they don't necessarily have to match the six habits above).

ⓜ Make the Move ⓜ

What habits would you like to have that would help you reach that six?	What existing habit can you stack this new one onto?
1.	
2.	
3.	
4.	
5.	
6.	

Building new habits is all about recognizing your strengths and weaknesses and building from there. By taking these six small steps above and applying great focus, your path to success will be clearer and brighter.

Sometimes the way seems insurmountably hard, and oppression weighs down the corners of our good intentions all too often. Every day, young people just like you are navigating the mirror maze of oppressive systems, experiencing hate, racism, homophobia, discrimination, or socioeconomic marginalization at school, at work, or in the streets. Chances are that you deal with these issues daily; they grind at your will, making you believe you can't fight back.

But you can. You have the power to stand up to these injustices by adopting powerful habits like recognizing your greatness and being unwilling to reduce yourself to just a rank-and-file member of the workforce, or like advocating for yourself and others' fair wages, and like respecting people of different races, genders, abilities, and sexual orientations. By tackling oppression directly and refusing to perpetuate it, you can help chip away at the forces that keep all disconnected youth down. Rise up!

4.5. Identifying Skills and How to Build Them

At this point, you're probably feeling confident with the idea of habits, and even have some habits you're looking to form. But what about those skills?

Whether the skill is public speaking or coding, we all have to start somewhere. You've probably heard that phrase a million times, but don't think that means you can sleep on it. Knowing that you'll start from the ground up is one of the most important things to keep in mind.

To get ahead in the working world, job skills are vital. According to ManpowerGroup's 2017 Talent Shortage Survey, 40% of employers internationally haven't been able to fill job openings.[13] A quarter of the global working population is between fifteen and twenty-four, but more than half—that's 73.3 million—are unemployed.[14] The problem? A shortage of applicants with both the soft and hard skills you need.

Soft skills are interpersonal qualities, or "people skills." Examples include work ethic, communication, etiquette, time management, and problem-solving abilities. Soft skills have to do with your ability to be a team player, keep a positive attitude, work well under pressure, and handle constructive criticism. They're often misinterpreted as personality traits and passed off as unlearnable, but just like any other skill, soft skills are things you have the power to master.

Hard skills are more objective and therefore easier to teach. You can get them through formal training and education to perform specific work. Examples include science, math, writing, engineering, language, and programming. Regardless of the job you're looking for, soft and hard skills are a must. Employers aren't just looking for one or the other. They're looking for the whole package, and that can be you.

How hirable you are is less about the skills you already have in hand and more about how willing and able you are to learn and grow.[15] If you want to make it, you must strive to keep developing those skills.

Skill mastery doesn't take place in the classroom. The best way to learn a skill is to go out and do it again and again. The first step: identify the skills you need to develop in the first place. The best way to know which skills suit your goals is by asking someone established in the industry you're interested in for help. Go pro! Why ask the advice of someone who doesn't know when you could get inside information from someone who excels in that field? No matter what job you're interested in (becoming a barber, a graphic designer, a doctor), speak to the person who others consider a pro. Don't undervalue your time by asking someone less qualified than the best.

Information gleaned directly from the pros is more impactful and relevant than any other source of labor market information. The problem is that very few adults consciously share this information, and young people forget to ask. Despite formal connections to gainfully employed parents, mentors, and relatives, youth aren't filled in on the skills needed for success. Without this information, young people are forced to rely on secondary sources that are often outdated or isolated from today's labor market dynamics, challenges, and changes.

Through Universal Success Habit Two—building connections—you can go with the pros. The power of connections can help you gain critical information about the skills needed for future labor market success and identify what skills you already have.

For entry-level jobs, you need general employability skills—the basics. It's also crucial that you can articulate that you have these skills and give employers evidence of it. These skills can range from basic writing skills to more attitudinal ones, like gelling with coworkers.

Demonstrating you have these skills can make or break both getting and keeping a job. Build connections with the pros and ask them what skills are important to have at the ground level. After that, it's on you to learn them. To get a basic idea of some skills to get to work on, check the appendix for a listing of entry-level skills every young adult should have.

4.6. An Eye on the Future

With A.I., smartphone advancements, virtual reality, and space travel, the world is changing quickly—so quickly that research reveals that a third of the skills needed for future jobs haven't even been embraced by today's labor market. Work as we know it is changing. It's no secret that robots will overtake certain jobs, but that doesn't mean we should throw our hands up and quit the game. Humans need to be around to perform a lot of the jobs machines can't do—[16] and you can step up to be that person.

In the next few years, these skills will be in high demand. Will you be ready?

Soft Skills

1. **Decision-making**
   A classic skillset, knowing how to make decisions effectively, analyze information, and make informed judgements will never be obsolete.[17]

2. **Cognitive flexibility**
   Even though this is a newcomer to the world of job skills, knowing how to examine several concepts simultaneously will be highly prized. Think of this like taking different threads of thought and being able to braid them together, switching between threads as needed.[18]

3. **Negotiating**
   As more people shift to contract work and our work community is more diverse than ever, computer, math, design, and arts industries will need employees to communicate with and influence others.[19]

4. **Emotional intelligence**
   As we discussed in chapter three, being able to manage your

own emotions and recognize the emotions of others is a skill that is creeping its way to the spotlight. Don't be left behind.[20]

5. **Coordination with others**
Tailoring things to accommodate others and promote collaboration is an increasingly valuable social skill as our global world gets smaller.

6. **Service**
Another social skill, this is the ability to actively seek ways to help others on the job. By showing up as an employee who's not afraid to go the extra mile, you become an invaluable asset in any company.[21]

7. **Creativity.**
Being an innovator will be one of the top job skills in the future. To make it, you will need to find creative ways to implement the latest concepts and technology in an evolving world.[22]

Hard Skills

1. **People management.**
This will be greatly valued in the media and energy industries, and involves the ability to hire, develop, and motivate employees.[23]

2. **Complex problem-solving**
As our lives become melded with technology, over a third of jobs will soon require the ability to solve intricate problems.[24]

3. **Critical thinking**
Being able to objectively analyze and evaluate an issue will always be a coveted skill, regardless of technological advancements down the line.[25]

4. **UX Design**
Meaning "user experience," this is a versatile skill seen as one of the top five skills to know as of 2019. Look for free introductory courses online if you're looking to be ahead of the curve in a multitude of fields.[26]

5. Artificial Intelligence.

Like it or not, robots and A.I. are here to stay. Get a leg up by learning about coding and how to work with the tech that's shaping all of our lives.[27]

6. Cloud Computing.

It's likely that you haven't seen a floppy disk, and chances are that you think CDs are obsolete. These days, it's all about what's on "the cloud."[28]

Now's your chance to reflect on your own skill set. Remember, there's no pressure to have these all just yet. Answer the questions below honestly and think about how to get the above skills and reach for that six.

Make the Move

Put a checkmark next to each of the ten skills you feel you already have.	If you don't yet have the skill, how can you get it?
Decision making _____	
Cognitive flexibility _____	
Negotiating _____	
People management _____	
Emotional intelligence _____	
Coordination with others _____	
Service _____	
Creativity _____	
Complex problem-solving _____	
Critical thinking _____	
UX Design _____	
Artificial Intelligence _____	
Cloud Computing _____	

Now that you have a handle on where you stand with those skills, let's dig into your mastery of some common soft and hard skills.

Make the Move
Key Skills Self-Evaluation

For each of these skills below, rate yourself from one to nine, with one being "I don't know a thing about this," and nine being, "I'm a rockstar."

Soft Skills

- Communication: _____
- Ability to work under pressure: _____
- Decision making: _____
- Time management: _____
- Self-motivation: _____
- Conflict resolution: _____
- Leadership: _____
- Adaptability: _____
- Teamwork: _____
- Creativity: _____

Hard Skills

- Science: _____
- Math: _____
- Writing: _____
- Engineering: _____
- Languages: _____
- Computer skills/coding: _____
- Typing: _____
- Construction/trade skills: _____
- Accounting: _____
- Design: _____

Identifying your key skills and abilities is crucial to getting the job you want. Now that you've completed this first evaluation, what strengths did you uncover?

_____

_____

What areas do you need to improve on the most?

_____

_____

For the skills you scored less than seven in, ask yourself if that skill (especially the hard skills) is one you should be focusing on developing to help you reach your goals—not all of them will apply to your dreams.

Reach out to one or two of your HUB members and a teacher about the self-evaluation you just did, and ask them to help you figure out if you're being too self-critical or if those really are areas you need to improve. Once you've identified a few core areas, ask them for advice on how to improve them. Write their suggestions down, plan them out, and see them through.

You're just beginning. Here's some advice for getting the ball rolling:

On-the-Job Training

If you're working, then you have a perfect opportunity at your feet to develop key skills. The company may offer formal training classes to their employees or sponsor you to take courses at a local community college. Speak to your personnel representative about your options. If there aren't any formal classes available, use work-related material to improve your basic skills. Read the instruction manuals, get comfortable with the computer systems, study and understand the ins and outs of your paycheck, and read the benefits manual. Try talking with someone at your company about ways to improve—you might learn that a manager will be thrilled that you took the time to ask. Try spending time with many different people in the company and get the scoop on how they operate, paying extra attention to employees who get along with others. What do they do? How do they respond to conflict? Copy their style and don't be too shy to ask for guidance.

Your job is your laboratory where you can test out new knowledge and skills. No matter your position, there's always an opportunity to learn.

School or Program Concentration
Ask a teacher or counselor to help you develop the skills you lack. If you're currently enrolled at school or in a skills-training program, you have a wonderful opportunity to use everything available to your advantage. In fact, those extra services are usually free. All you need to do is take initiative and show your motivation. Daily practice is a good place to start. Just like playing a sport, the more you do it, the better you'll get. The only difference is that you have a greater chance of achieving success through work and school than you do in sports.

Improving Writing Skills
This skill is vital, and getting a foothold in improving it is free. Try picking a favorite song or rap verse and writing down the words, then rewrite each sentence so it's grammatically correct. You can also start your own newsletter to keep the members of your HUB up-to-date, then use these newsletters in your portfolio. Reach out to a teacher or well-read adult to work with you on this. If you're eying an entry-level job in a field you're interested in, or if you want to go to college, practice writing personal statements and cover letters using free prompts you can find online.

Improving Math Skills
To improve your math skills, there's no better place than working out your personal budget. Practice by laying out a full budget based on the following salaries: $8, $15, or $20 an hour. Calculate weekly, monthly, and yearly pay for forty hours of work a week. Be sure to take out the 15% federal taxes. Try itemizing your spending down to the smallest item.
Next, look up the minimum wage in your state and do it all again. How much can you save in each income bracket? Where do you want to be financially?

Improving Communications Skills
If possible, record a video of yourself. Make a five-minute presentation introducing yourself, your interests, and your goals. Be as interesting,

informative, and direct as possible. This is invaluable interview prep. Look for articles online on communication strategies for making friends. Pick up a book at the library on the topic. Answers are out there—just get looking!

There are hundreds of other ways to improve your skills if you put your mind to it. Although we haven't yet mentioned the importance of a resume, good interviewing techniques, and proper gear (and we're not talking Yeezy sneakers and a hoodie), we aren't saying those don't matter. At the library, the bookstore, or the internet, you can find a hundred sources on the basics of job hunting. When you combine our specific techniques with basic job search skills, success is sure to follow you.

4.7. Ongoing Evaluation

We've created a Daily Self-Evaluation Sheet to help you hone your self-analysis and examination skills. Being able to give yourself honest feedback is crucial. Shoot for a daily self-evaluation for the next six months. This evaluation is based on the six universal habits that we know lead to making it. You don't need to speak the King's English to succeed. You don't need to know how to perform complex mathematical equations either. All you need to do is stay alive, free, and focused.

Remember, the key to building great skills and habits is by employing the 2/1/30 Rule: two new skills and one new habit every thirty days. We acquire skills through training and formal education. On the other hand, habits can be incorporated by developing a growth mindset and through habit stacking. Every thirty days, focus on the development of two new skills and one new habit that has your life, freedom, and future economic opportunity in mind.

At the end of the book, we provide you with a blank evaluation tool for your continued use. Once you master the self-evaluation process, you can modify it to suit your own needs.

The Daily Process will go like this: at the end of each day, reflect on the effort you put in toward making it, using the form. Some days will be easier than others—that's okay. Just keep on the path and you'll soon be enjoying habits and skills that have you steadily rowing toward that six.

At the end of the week, add up your daily scores, then divide by seven to get the weekly point total. That'll help you have a good idea of how your success journey is going overall. For weekly scores under two, reach out to a HUB member or other positive person in your life for advice and suggestions. Add these to next week's goals and keep your board members updated on your progress; they're a resource and may have ideas or suggestions.

Daily Self-Evaluation Key				
5 – Outstanding	4 – Good	3 – Satisfactory	2 – Needs Improvement	1 – Unsatisfactory

Self-Evaluation

Mon._____ Tues._____ Wed._____ Thurs._____ Fri._____ Sat._____ Sun._____

Daily Self-Evaluation

1. How did I develop my interviewing skills today?

Action:

_____

_____

_____

Barriers/Challenges:

_____

_____

Recommendations:

_____

_____

2. How did I dress for the success I want?

Action:

_____

_____

_____

Barriers/Challenges:

_____

_____

Recommendations:

_____

_____

3. How well did I let things go?

Action:

_____

_____

_____

Barriers/Challenges:

_____

_____

Recommendations:

_____

_____

Overall Score for the Day: _____

Fill this form out every day, adapting your three questions to reflect your monthly skills and habits you're working to acquire. Practicing 2/1/30 and holding yourself accountable will revolutionize your future economic opportunity. Carrying weapons, starting fistfights, or dealing drugs will destroy your economic future; education and training can only enhance it. It's important that your 2/1/30 routine is focused on getting you past the Urban Survival Syndrome.

Self-evaluation is a powerful experience and this skill will last you a lifetime. All successful people and organizations take the time to see how they can improve. By doing the same, you are not only on the path to success, you're also engaging in the same quality management practices used by corporations. At your next interview, throw in some information about how you do regular self-evaluation and watch how quickly you make it on the payroll.

So what two skills and one habits are you starting today?

Skill:_____ **Skill:**_____ **Habit:**_____

Sometimes it's the journey that teaches you a lot about your
destination.

- Drake

UNIVERSAL SUCCESS HABIT FIVE:

Successful Young Adults Consistently Decode Power, Privilege, and Injustice in a Way That Helps Them Overcome Any Barriers to Their Success.

Mariela scrolled through her Instagram, struggling to focus her eyes on her feed. She'd had too much to drink—again—and as she ambled home, she'd kicked at stray beer cans and felt disappointment coursing through her body. It wasn't just because her friend's dad had come home from work early, breaking up their party. It was what he'd said to her that hurt: "My daughter shouldn't be hanging around trash like you."

Trash? When had she suddenly become trash? She was in her junior year, but inside, she still felt like the kid in Ms. Henderson's computer class in fourth grade, running her fingers over the keys, so sure that she'd found her thing: computers. Mariela kept scrolling, ignoring the word "trash" in her head, remembering the programs and games she used to mess around on as a kid. Technology had made sense to her, and she'd lay in bed thinking about the games she'd be making one day, but when she tried to talk to someone about her goals, she came up empty-handed—especially when she'd bounce ideas off of her older sister, Dee. She seemed focused on just about everything besides ideas and plans: parties, boys, drinking.

It didn't help that their mom was always busy working late shifts at the restaurant and left her under her sister's care so often. When all Mariela saw was Dee living one big party, the computer looked less and less appealing, and her sister looked like she was having the time of her life. Mariela slowly found herself falling into circles like her sister's, and that drive to enjoy the moment started chipping away at her longing to plan for her future beyond just next week. Even though she fiddled around on the family computer sometimes, her daydreams about the future eventually started to fade. Mariela never forgot the moment that sealed the nail in the coffin for her: in eighth grade, Mariela had been steadily putting her energy into her computer class and her teacher had encouraged her to join the weekly STEM club. On the first Wednesday meeting, Mariela opened the classroom door to a room filled with white boys armed with their own laptops. Mariela's fingers clenched around the beat up three-ring binder she'd brought with her for notes, every neck craned to watch her. Only the teacher seemed unphased, excited to have "a fresh face" in the club, ushering her in. However, once they started on the month's new project, it was clear that a laptop was necessary. Now, Mariela's family had just the one, and her mom had said it was too special to leave the house. The teacher smiled, "No worries! Mariela, work with Jay over there. I can bring you one to borrow next week."

To her left, Jay sat with a sneer plastered on his face, eyes flickering over Mariela before landing on the teacher. "Mr. Benson, she's a girl! What's she doing here?" He slouched in his chair. "Do I really have to work with her?" Tears welled in Mariela's eyes, and a horrified Mr. Benson tried to smooth it over, but before he could say more than a few sentences, Mariela gathered up her binder and stormed out.

After that, she was pretty set in her sister's ways. Anyway, it wasn't like her sister got too much flak in her own life, and each time she tried to pursue computers it was like reaching a wall—money, boys, feeling like a fish out of water. It wasn't until she was sixteen that she realized something had to give.

Around that time, Mariela fell in with a new boyfriend: Mike. He was cute, he always knew where the booze was, and he lived for the now. Even though he knew nothing about her old love of technology and never asked serious questions about her life, he was nice enough, and after watching her aunt spend decades trapped with a husband who hit her, she considered herself lucky. Finding someone "nice enough" like Mike wasn't always easy.

One Wednesday, after Mike had convinced Mariela and their friends to skip, a cop car rolled up on them drinking in an alley off Colfax. An officer took Mariela back home, and her mom's face sank when she took in the sight of Mariela with an officer behind her.

"You were so smart, Mari. What happened to you?"

Mariela had no answer and instead hung her head, so ashamed she couldn't breathe. When her court date arrived, Mariela lucked out. She hadn't been caught drinking before then and only got slapped with community service…and a court fine her family couldn't quite afford.

In the weeks that followed, Mariela's free time was swallowed by her community service time and helping out around the house extra—her mom had to take on three extra shifts to cover the fine and came home sore after working doubles. While fixing her mom something easy for a late dinner, Mariela thought about her situation and her family. She loved her mom, admired her work ethic, but didn't want to spend her life like swollen-footed and smelling like cooking grease. Glancing through the kitchen door, she eyed the computer in the corner of the room. She used to be so sure about what she wanted, and now it seemed so beyond her.

Her phone buzzed. It was Mike, asking her to go out and drink with him. Again. He'd already brushed off his community service. "It's a joke, babe. Total waste of my time." She ignored Mike's text and went over to the computer, starting it up and spending the night cleaning the hard drive and installing updates. The next morning, she broke up with Mike and approached one of her teachers, Mr. Martel, who ran the STEM club and told him she was interested in joining. "But," she added, "I can't bring a computer or anything."

"That's okay. Just bring yourself and we'll go from there. Can you come to tomorrow's meeting? We're starting a new topic."

He seemed so easy about it, so sure it would be fine. The next day, she stood outside the classroom with her heart in her throat and her *same three-ring binder, now taped in different parts, in front of her chest. When she opened the door, the club's conversation lulled briefly as heads turned to assess the new arrival. A sea of about fifteen faces swam before her, mostly boys, but this time they weren't all white—and there was one other girl there to boot. She still felt out of her element and knew most of the other students saw her as a party girl, but she knew this was where she belonged. She looked at them all, hoping they weren't judging her sudden decision to join them despite the hobbies they all knew her for. Someone broke the silence.*

"There's a free seat over here," one of the young men waved her over. She sank down in the seat next to him and he smiled at her, sticking out his hand. "Dante."

She smiled back. "Mariela."

After that, Mariela fell into an easy friendship with Dante and the only other girl in the club, Leeann. With the two of them, she felt sure of herself and her purpose. And even though she had terrible grades from those past few years partying, Mariela decided to try to apply to college. The only problem was actually applying—nobody in her family had done it. But Dante's family had, and with his mom's help, Mariela applied to a community college, snagging the financial aid she needed thanks to being a first gen student. Within 2 years, Mariela had her AAS in coding. Now, at age 21, she works in a tech company, pouring her passion into her job. In the evenings, she works at a weekly coding camp for teen girls, fighting to break the cycle of oppression and share the life she worked so hard for.

What exactly changed Mariela's life?

By learning to code, she actually learned how to decode—how to tap into the flow of social structures, expectations, and barriers around her to navigate success. By taking an honest look at the misrepresenters around her, the way how spent her free time, and the powers, privileges, and injustices at play that kept her back, she was able to make the changes she needed to live the life she truly deserved. Reflecting and decoding gave her the space to change, and because of it, she found her way out of her family's snare of poverty, drinking, and domestic violence.

Through taking those steps towards her six, Mariela brought others along. When Dee saw her sister revolutionize her life, she realized she had to make a change, too, and is now enrolled in Project Code Switch, a local program that prepares young adults for a career as a tech support analyst, based on Mariela's advice. Thanks to her social capital, Mariela will be able to help Dee get a job when the program is completed. Mike is doing better as well. After Mariela started making changes, he came over to her house and they talked honestly for the first time about feelings and ambitions; they're still friends today. Her steps inspired him, and although his computer passions are only in Fruity Loops (the music production software), he started taking his interests seriously and just landed his first entry gig helping book rappers and electronic artists at an underground music venue.

The best thing about Mariela's story is that it's easier to learn to do what she did than you think. The key that separates successful young people from the pack is Universal Success Habit Five: **consistently decoding the system.**

5.1. Adapt and Evolve

While this book won't teach you the tricks of coding, it can train you on decoding the people, places, and things misrepresenting true survival and future economic opportunity. Although we may all be created equally on principle, the sad truth is that our country doesn't provide opportunity in equal measures to all its citizens. Homophobia, racism, and sexism all play roles in keeping people locked in a game of power, privilege, and injustice. Because of that, some people have been raised with the ins and outs of decoding in their back pocket while others have to wade through murky territory before beginning to learn techniques for decoding. But just because you have to work harder to reach the information that others have been born into doesn't mean you can't still strive for that six. With decoding, you'll be able to lock in that delayed-results mindset while turning away from the immediate-results snares that the systems, people, and places in your life have been misdirecting you toward.

You've got a lot of promise; to take it to the next level, you must adapt and evolve. Remember: people who learn by trial and error will always lose to those who learn from others' trial and error. By watching the actions and missteps of others, the way to success clears up. By decoding the system that way, you'll figure out which people and organizations in your city or town are the keepers of the keys to your success, which of those are passionate about empowering folks who aren't in power positions, and how to navigate through the social settings where they don't care a bit about the empowerment of others.[1]

Today is a new day. Stop and breathe. You don't have to learn for yourself; just look around you. The information is all already there, waiting for you to grab hold of it.

5.2. Find Your Why

We said it back in 4.7, and we'll say it again: when you lock in on the why, things get easier. With your why, you start decoding the misrepresenters that lead you toward the one. Envisioning your dreams and goals renders them powerless. When you have your eyes on true survival, it's easier to turn toward the representers who can lead you to the six. And who knows? Maybe your actions will inspire your misrepresenters. Maybe your today could be their tomorrow.

All misrepresenters, whether oppressive social structures or specific individuals, have been playing games on you and your freedom, and you may get angry when you look around and see that some people your age have been given all the resources to uncover their why obstacle-free. Being angry is okay. Just don't give up on yourself. Instead, work every day towards that six—and teach others how to do the same if you're inspired to.

All we ask is that you go into these new habits with ease because you're still going. Just like Jordan, you may have missed more than nine thousand shots and lost over three hundred games, but you know that doesn't mean the game is over.[2] You've always got another move. Show up every day and live like you're in love with opportunity, and it won't be long until opportunity falls in love with you back.

It's not just your own survival that hinges on your ability to decode, but it's also the progress of your community and others who share your identity. There always has to be a first: the first trans woman on the cover of a fashion magazine, the first woman of color in space, the first African-American president. Why can't that first be you?

It may seem hard; most times, it can be a struggle just to figure out how to decode. Shifting your thinking may sound easier said than done, but in the long run, decoding is far simpler than continuing to plow down a reckless path that leads you away from your six. You already have the best tool for success in your corner, and it's one that nobody can take away from you: the power of your mind.

The first important step in decoding is realizing your path is by no means fixed. None of it has been decided already. It's in your hands to push towards the six, and your success depends on your focus. If you plan to escape the traps that your current life has sprung, it's essential. Looking around, it can be easy to see others—city workers, teachers, entrepreneurs—and assume they always had it easy, but often, that couldn't be further from the truth.

Many adults had to take the same steps you're taking right now in order for a lightbulb to start blinking over their heads. They didn't come into adulthood with all the answers, and many of them had to totally revolutionize how they were approaching their lives (and often at a price). Hardship succeeded in changing them where courts or parents couldn't, and after struggling down dark roads for years, they found their way out of the woods.

How can you tap into that life you want sooner rather than later? How do you avoid the pitfalls that tripped up the people before you and cement that delayed-results mindset? By committing to your own success. And to get there, you have to decode each facet of your life.

PEOPLE, POLICIES, AND SYSTEMS

5.3. Friends – not Forever

Friends: the ones we make now will last forever, right?

Wrong.

Look, at the beginning of this book, we promised to keep it real with you, and we're going to see that through even when the truth stings. Part of MAKiN iT is keeping it one hundred. And we've put a lot of work into figuring out what it takes to really make it out there.

Here's the truth, flat-out: possibly the biggest factor in your success is your social circle (those friends you see day after day). According to a study done by Florida Atlantic University in Miami, only 1% of all friendships started between the ages of twelve and thirteen even survive five years.[3]

Just one percent.

A 1% shot that 100% determines your future. Even if you're a little older than that, the likelihood that the friendships you're investing in now will become part of your forever crew is real low. But the impact those friendships have on the rest of your life? That's real, and potentially permanent. Who you choose to hang around with now can ripple into your adulthood, impacting opportunities and decisions down the road long after those people have moved on. If you're building relationships with people who drag you and your dreams down, it's likely both you and your crew will suffer from the choices made together long after that friendship has run its course. Remember: if you follow, their today may be your tomorrow.

Sound like a lot? What if we flip it on its head? Hanging out with people who encourage you, motivate you, and push you toward the six impacts your success and happiness down the line—even if that friendship also fizzles out. Before you beat yourself up over the friendships you've been forging up until now, remember how much time you have ahead of you, and recognize that there are things beyond your control that contribute to why you may not be rating yourself as high on the survival scale as you'd like. Like we said in 3.5, your ability to totally reason and judge doesn't even solidify until your mid-twenties – research tells us that your brain hasn't finished building bridges that connect actions to consequences just yet, leaving you vulnerable to peer pressure.

That's why the most powerful influence in your life is your peer group, even more than your teachers. If you want to make it (and let's get real, you do), you have to brush shoulders with other people who are striving for something great.

5.4. Policies

Biology isn't the only thing to blame for your social circle leading you from the six, however. Have you ever stopped to think about why you hang out with the people you do? It isn't all by conscious choice. Although the U.S. officially ended segregation over sixty years ago, it's still alive and well in many forms today in schools, neighborhoods, and social circles. New research has come out in the past few years showing that institutionally and systematically, our school system is getting more segregated, both by race and by income, leaving the poorest schools to students of color, and the better funded schools to white, wealthier students. When there are less resources available in a school, they don't have the resources like up-to-date computers, quality creative funding, or scientific instruments available to give students an edge when pursuing their futures—and the cycle of keeping marginalized communities down continues. In fact, the problem seems to be spiraling: between 1996 and 2016, the number of segregated schools—where less than 40% of students were white—doubled.[4]

And it's not just school where this is happening. Our neighborhoods and communities mirror these statistics: 39.4% of minorities still find themselves in segregated neighborhoods. These statistics aren't just about diversity. When white people have historically been offered more privileges, higher salaries, and better job opportunities since our country was founded, the impact of segregated neighborhoods still keeps communities of color back: while about 72% of white households own homes, only 57% of Asian households, 48% of Hispanic households, and 42% of black households own homes as well.[5] That's a huge gap when we're talking about having secure housing and owning something as fundamental to the "American Dream" as your own home.

It keeps on rippling out, though, all the way out to the lack of diversity in our social groups. According to a shocking 2014 study, 75% of white American don't have any non-white friends.[6] You read that correctly. While white Americans historically have access to higher pay, easier access to home ownership, and better future economic opportunities from the get-go, most of the time that means they're only sharing their wealth of knowledge and social capital with other white people. While this isn't necessarily carried out on purpose by individuals, the legal barriers from our shared past that kept us separated from each other haven't yet been undone, leaving us with an imbalance in access to vital resources.

What does this all mean for you? Let's find out.

Make the Move

1. What marginalized or oppressed groups do you identify with? This can be your race, gender identity, sexual orientation, income, ability, mental health status, education, religion, or first language.

_____

_____

_____

2. What are the ways discrimination and segregation have limited your resources? Take some time to think about this one, combing through all of your identities. It may be in more ways than you think.

_____

_____

_____

_____

_____

3. Are there specific policies or systems that have marginalized ("othered") you? If so, which ones?

_____

_____

_____

4. How about individual people or places that have marginalized you?

_____

_____

5. Who are people you know, either in the real world, online, or celebrities/public figures, who have similar backgrounds to you and seem to have overcome the effects of marginalization? Write the names of five people, and beside them on each line, write what they did to get there.

1. _____

2. _____

3. _____

4. _____

5. _____

If possible, reach out to the people you know who overcame the effects of segregation and marginalization and ask about how they did it. If you don't know anyone in person, Instagram and other websites are brimming with folks eager to talk about their own success within the crossroads of their own identities.

Jot down any information you learn from them right here:

_____

_____

_____

_____

_____

_____

_____

_____

_____

_____

Keep those connections, and don't be afraid to ask for more insight. The best way to learn how to decode is by asking the people like you who have successfully decoded to get where they are now.

5.5. Stacked Against Us

Successful young people, especially young people who face discrimination, know that education isn't the only thing necessary for building that FEO, let alone securing an equal place at the table. It takes more than just that degree to up your income, and the statistics we talked about in the last section only serve to make some people's degrees financially worth more than others. The statistics don't lie: recent research has shown that African American families whose head earned a college degree only have 2/3 of the wealth of white families headed by a high school dropout.[7]

The case isn't much better for people in trade programs, either. A recent study came out that found African American men who took part in apprenticeships earned an average of just $14.35 after completing their program while their white peers earned about $26.14;[8] these disparities stem from many factors, including the segregation we talked about in 5.4. This overwhelming gap costs more than just your wallet, too. Researchers at Arizona State University recently showed that traditionally marginalized youth who grew up taught the American ideal—that hard work and perseverance naturally and always lead to success—have a drop in self-esteem and a rise in risky behavior during middle school.[9] Of course people will be discouraged on their road to the six when the American Dream has been fed to all Americans yet is only accessible to some. To make matters even muddier, people who really believe the system is fair internalize stereotypes about themselves and others—believing and acting out false and negative claims about their group—more readily than those who disavow these views.[10] By simply believing these negative things, you could be setting yourself down a path you didn't need to take in the first place.

Don't go enrolling in a program just yet, thinking you'll at least be earning more money than you were before. While the possession of a degree will increase your earning potential, the inequality gap between white and black college graduates is greater than the wealth gap between white and black high school dropouts. If you're black, the more education you receive, the greater the wealth disparity will be between you and your white peers. How do you make it in the face of all this? By taking a step back—that immediate-results mentality goes both ways when it comes to guiding you to make the wrong decisions. Blindly enrolling in college and maxing out loans in the name of "making it" could cost you not only financially but also in opportunity cost. The time you spend in college chasing down a degree you may never get (or the degree that's undervalued in the labor market) may not outweigh the benefits of securing a short-term credential (like a trade) while building social capital and skills up in the labor market.

If you really want to make it, it's less about whether you go to college and more about how you do it. Did you know that most high school graduates go on to some form of post-secondary education, but half don't receive any marks of completion? Or that only 28% of community college students graduate in four years? For four-year students degree programs, only 60% graduate within six years. Our college dropout rate in this country is worse than most inner-city public high rates.[11]

Don't shut this book thinking college isn't the answer; know that attending college without a plan in mind, and without social capital, isn't some magic ticket on the road to MAKiN iT. Get a plan, make connections, and find out which program is best for you and what systems are in place for your success.

Remember: people who learn from trial and error will always lose to those who learn from others' trial and error. Instead of plowing in without a plan, learn from others. You'll be glad you did.

Make the Move

Find six two or four-year graduates with similarities in background to you. You can do this through the internet, meetups, old friends, friends' families, or teachers. Get to know them and use the chance to pick their brains about how they made it. Who knows, these college graduates could be part of your hub.

Ask them these questions:

1. How did you know which courses to choose?
   a. Which courses did you choose? Which ones do you recommend?
   b. Are there any you wish you hadn't taken?

2. What are your tips for choosing a college?
   a. What do you wish you'd known that you know now?
   b. What was the hardest part about applying to college? The easiest?
   c. Do you like your college? Why/why not?
3. What habits have helped you do well?
   a. What habits did you have to kick?
   b. What did you learn your final year of college you wish you'd learned your first year?
4. How did you not fall through the cracks?
   a. What groups did you join?
   b. What resources were there that helped you?
   c. What resources did you not know about until too late that you wish you'd known about earlier?

Asking people who have made it before you will help make the way clearer. You got this.

5.6. Connections Before the Credentials

So how do you go through the obstacle course of social capital when some people are making ten dollars more per hour than you from the outset? It's all about setting up those valuable connections before starting a program. Once you find your passion—your "why"—start building connections in that industry right away. When those connections have your back, you have insight on the program or school's reputation within your specific industry.

Knowing how to establish connections is a critical piece in the earning puzzle. Before starting a program, build connections in the industry you're drawn to. Having the right connections in hand can give you insight about the best programs or schools for your focus—and which ones have the students' futures in mind. Because while educational and workforce programs may be drawing you in to earn that credential or secure a degree, they aren't all equally committed to helping you make the connections needed to put that diploma or certificate to work. Strong connections are more valuable than the credential itself; without those links, it's hard to put your achievement to work, grinding you down financially and mentally.

Make the Move

Dream Job or industry?	What connections do you have in this industry?	How close are you on a scale of 1 to 6?	How can you make new connections or deepen them?	What is a number, email, or address for someone you can talk to in that field?

When you do contact an employer or connection, ask them these questions:

1. Where do most of your employees graduate or receive their certificate from?

2. What are you looking for when hiring people who have just graduated/gotten their certificate, but have little work experience?

3. What is your number one piece of advice for getting ahead in this field?

When you've gotten a few schooling recommendations, reach out to the programs (reaching out in person is the best way), and ask them these questions:

1. Where do the majority of your graduates find employment?

2. What type of support do you provide in connecting students with industry professionals while they're in the program?

3. May I have the contact information of a few employers to speak to them about your program?

You'll be surprised how happy people are to help young adults get their bearings when trying to seek out credentials.

5.7. Who's Reppin' the Six?

It doesn't matter if it's people, policies, or attitudes holding you back, it's time to let them go. Now don't go set this book down and break up with your significant other or shut down a campus office just yet but do hold whatever's coming up for you in the back of your mind as you work through this chapter. You'll have plenty of time to make those changes once you're armed with the tools and knowledge at hand.

If you're serious about shining, checking who you're running with and where you find yourself hanging is a good place to start, but you need to take a hard look at your life. Sometimes these things run deep, and the policies, people, and habits around us can burrow like a cancer, ruining every aspect of your life. Do the people, policies, and things you surround yourself with push you toward the six, or are they infecting your life and holding you back?

Successful young adulting depends on your ability to be honest with yourself and the roles others play in your life. Thriving young people recognize the need to prioritize their best interests. By personally realizing and embracing this independence from their social circle, you're helping more than yourself: your work actually helps your old friends think over what's best for them. Don't be influenced any longer—be the influencer instead. If you see your friends heading down a dangerous path, don't follow. Turn around and walk in the other direction. You'll be surprised how many friends will want to follow you.

If you do find people giving you grief for making these changes or resisting your life choices, take a step back and evaluate. Are these people actually your friends? For that matter, what does it even mean to be a good friend? Look over the forces in your life and assess who's got you (and who's trying to hold you back).

In the chart below, write down ten major players in your life. Who do you spend the most time with? Who influences you the most? Is it a system or place instead of a person? Write them all down—and be honest with yourself!

Once you've written down your ten, put a check next to their name in the "reppin'" or "misreppin'" column, depending on whether that force promotes your life, freedom, and economic opportunities or not. Remember, a force absolutely can't do both. If someone tells you they've got your back right before helping you jump someone, that's not long-term survival—that's misrepresenting.

Make the Move

Forces	Reppin'	Misreppin'

Once you've done this for all ten people, multiply the total checks in the "reppin'" column by ten (that's the number of names listed).

(checks in the reppin' column) _____ x 10 = _____%

That percentage above is your MAKiN iT percentage—what percent of your top ten forces have your true survival, your six, in mind. If your percentage is less than eighty, you need to do some soul searching about your social priorities. Think about it: would you hop into a car if the driver leaned out the window and said, "Don't sweat, we got a 70% chance of this car not killing us?" I didn't think so.

Many young people don't work on decoding their environment because most young adults have not been taught how or supported in doing so, especially with the systems of privilege, power, and institutionalized racism at play. You're getting the tools right here—now make that change and up your MAKiN iT percentage to get you to that six.

5.8. Associations of Convenience

All this unpacking segregation and oppression and how it relates to privileges, power, and injustice probably has you realizing that most friendships aren't true friendships. Instead, they're associations of convenience. You and your friends have been brought together by factors you didn't think you had control over: racial discrimination, your neighborhood, your income levels, your schools. Sometimes the way you meet your "friends" happens because of something as basic as the first letter of your last names landing you in the same homeroom.

We just keep seeing these people because it's easy, even if that someone is helping us justify actions that keep us spiraling toward danger. It's that immediate-result environment again, pushing us to keep doing what's easy. When you're just skating by, moment to moment, convenience takes over and leaves you high and dry when you need to make moves promoting your life, freedom, and FEO.

If you're still unsure if someone's your true friend or just an association of convenience, test it out: using those ten people on the list above, imagine if you asked them to help you figure out how to succeed. Their answers will tell you everything you need to know. Would they tell you to get your grades up and go to college, or move products on the streets?

What about the forces on your list that are systems, policies, or places? Imagine if you went to someone who worked in that force's office and told them about your goals. Would they be showing you how to navigate the policies and obstacles, or would they be pushing you to quit or figure it out yourself?

If these forces are giving you tools or inspiration for improvement, then that force is more than just a convenient association. But if one of those ten gave you dangerous advice or closed the door in your face, then they're just trying to take the quick path out and are eager to have another person justify their pursuit of the wrong direction or their discriminatory practices.

Stick to the forces pushing you to be your best self. They're strong; breaking free from the snares society has set for us is hard. Striving to help other people succeed is even harder. But acting a fool—that's easy. The choice is in your hands.

Make the Move

What would it look like if you valued your true survival instead of settling for convenience? Use all five senses to describe how your life would be different:

What would you see around you?

_____

_____

What would you physically feel?

_____

_____

What could you hear?

_____

_____

What would you smell?

_____

_____

What would you taste?

_____

_____

Setting out on the road to your success can be tough. If it weren't, we wouldn't need this book; everyone would just march on toward bright futures by waking up and breathing the air. Remember, it's not that you don't know how to make it. Clues and examples are everywhere—even reading this book is a huge step you're taking to make it.

If you looked over your list of ten forces and thought none of them would encourage you to apply to college or a post-educational program, or that they'd laugh at your wildest ambitions, start thinking on how you can be the inspiration yourself. We can sit around waiting for someone to break us out of our money, race, gender, and class traps until we're dead, or we can be the person we've been waiting for and set our own selves free.

What'll you choose?

5.9. Parents: They Lost Their Way

For better or worse, our parents' attitudes and behaviors shape us into the adults we become, but sometimes the path they lay out isn't one to true survival. Parents pushing us towards the one is harder to cope with than friends or acquaintances. They swear they love their children, yet at the same time can become abusive, prioritize drugs, get locked up, or disappear on the family without notice. Trauma hoisted onto you by your parents can be so painful and so intense that it can be hard to see how to make it clearly when your life is so wrapped up in theirs. Someone's saying they love you doesn't necessarily mean they're good for you. It can be those people who tell you they love you the most that are dragging you toward the darkest dangers.

If family is hurting you most, it can be hard to figure out what to do. Leaving home often only makes it worse, especially if you're under eighteen. That's where your friends—your chosen family—come in. Find people who are helping you succeed and spend your free time with the friends dedicated to promoting your and their life, freedom, and FEO.

Building up your FEO gets you out from under the thumb of needing food, clothing, and shelter from toxic households. In the meantime, there are ways to get out of the house and work on empowering yourself to move onward and upward sooner rather than later, but where do you go when you need to get away?

5.10.   Where You Go

Places

If your family is part of the trap that's keeping you back, it's often not enough to just escape the house for the day. Leaving without a purpose can land you in places as dangerous as before—or worse. When home isn't a space you can bloom in, it's even more critical to find healthier places to hang out.

You aren't alone. With a few key strategies, you can rethink the places you're spending most of your time and where you need to be to make it.

Even just deciding to revamp your social circle is a huge step, and you should feel proud of that decision. But if you change the faces around you while visiting the same old haunts from before, get ready for some disappointment. Stick around the same places, and you'll end up with a new crew as uninterested in succeeding as the last, landing right back at square one.

Below, write the five places where you spend most of your time. To the right, write down why you spend your time there. What about that place draws you back again and again? Finally, put a checkmark under "reppin'" or "misreppin'." Just like people and systems, a place can't be both. Which of these places offer success and FEO-building? Do any of them line up with those ambitions you visualized earlier in the chapter?

Make the Move

Places	Why here?	Reppin'	Misreppin'

For those places that are misreppin,' where could you go instead? If you've got a few places here (e.g. an aunt's house that is safe, for example), then that's a good start. If you listed school as one of those five places, then your next moves should be a breeze. Joining a club or sport at your school is an excellent way to align your social circle with your goals and a sure way to spend time in places that nourish your mind, body, and spirit. What would you do if nothing—no systems, no money, no people—were holding you back? Want to play sports? Join a team. Fascinated by computers or science? Sign up for the STEM or Robotics club. Looking to be the next Will Smith or Gina Rodriguez? Get involved in the drama club. Everybody great has started somewhere small, so get started. That somewhere for you can be as easy as an after-school club.

These places aren't just for building skills. When you're hanging out in the wrong places, the wrong opportunities come for you, but if you're putting time and energy into a place aligned with the same goals you're striving for, then opportunities that crop up will be in line with your dreams. It's never too early to start building your social capital, making relationships and experiences that will help you unlock your dream job down the line. When you're in the right place, you just keep meeting new people until the right one comes along.

Take a young woman named Erin as an example. She dropped out of high school, got wrapped up in drugs, and had a rough ten years as a single mom of two. One day, she realized she'd had enough and applied to her dream program: mortuary school. Even with a criminal record, she was offered an entry-level job at a funeral home when she visited the school's open house—even before starting classes. Often, the people who are the doers and makers in the places you start spending time can sense when they've stumbled across a driven young person and are eager to help you out. You just need to put yourself in a place for those successful people to find you and take you under their wing.

If you aren't in school, you still have options. The internet is one amazing tool for finding events, virtual spaces, and physical venues that line up with your ambitions. Even if you don't have access to a computer at home, make the trek to the library and use one of their computers. They're free and open to the public—all you need is a library card. When you get online, look for organized social groups instead of surfing Tumblr or Instagram or Facebook. If you want to be a writer, hang out with other writers in a workshop. If you're looking to learn how to code, find a free class or library group to learn how.

Community-building and success cannot happen in a bubble. You've got to put yourself in a space that has the community you need for success, and it takes work. You've got these tools, so think: where would you go if nobody could stop you? Imagine what it would look like to already be there, setting off on your best life. The first step doesn't begin at old stomping grounds; it starts somewhere new. It's up to you to figure out where that somewhere is.

Finding places where you can build your social capital and hustle for your goals is key— job fairs, libraries, clubs, meetups, and programs are all great ways to start. If you're old enough, a job can help you focus and make the money you need to plan for the future, and if your home situation is unsafe, these healthy and productive reasons for getting out of the house help you make it through until you can get out on your own safely.

Make the Move

List 5 places you can go that rep your life, freedom, and FEO.
1.
2.
3.
4.
5.

You've got to eliminate all the dangerous places, people, and things that are serving as roadblocks, but be careful. The immediate-results mindset will whisper in the back of your head, urging you to keep those dangerous elements in your life, encouraging you to return to those same old places that never served your goals. Whenever that voice does pop up—and it will—take a breath and think: does the place you used to go promote your life, freedom, or FEO? If the answer is no, then it isn't contributing to your survival. Not by a long shot.

The power is in your hands to make a difference. Where can you go to further your dreams and build the social capital that supports you?

5.11. Filling Your Hours

Things

Now that you're clued in on the places, people, and systems that serve your goals, there's a third item to decode if you're really going to get that next level: the things that you own or do and how they fill up the hours in your day.

What are you doing when you're not in school or at work? Scrolling through your phone? Drinking and smoking with friends? When was the last time you worked on a creative project for fun or tried to learn a new skill? If it's been a long time—or never—you need to seriously reevaluate. What's taking up the space in your calendar, and what is it keeping you from doing? What if you spent time each day working toward something you want to do in the long run and not just seeking instant gratification? If you want to be more athletic, work out or pick up a sport. If you want to be a better musician, dust off your guitar or download Garageband.

How can that list of places you wrote help you swap the things clogging up your hours? The library is a great place to borrow books on topics you want to learn about, and many libraries offer free classes on everything from Excel to poetry to 3D printing. Most successful people didn't wake up at five years old knowing exactly what they wanted to do with their life; they struggled to carve out some meaning, trying out different skills or projects until they found one that felt right for them. If one new thing doesn't pan out, don't give up. Investing your energy into events and workshops that further—or simply identify—your dreams is the key to success. You're already on the right track. Keep going.

Getting a job is a great way to establish independence and stability. We'll tell it to you straight, though: you won't get your dream job out the gate (nobody does), but you'll meet people and gain knowledge that will help you work your way toward a job that funds your dreams, until eventually, you're earning money off your goals alone. To get the ball rolling, find a job that has hours that work for you and gives you the chance to meet people who are invested in your well-being. Getting a job and working hard at it makes a world of difference and gives you a huge boost in both social capital and establishing places that support your life, freedom, and FEO.

. But there's more to it than just that. When you do earn that paper in your first job, it's normal to be pumped and buy silly things for yourself—and that's fine in moderation. But once you start blowing it on dangerous things like alcohol, drugs, and cigarettes, stop and think. What if, instead of buying that bottle of whiskey, you bought something you needed for an art or music project? Saved up for that laptop or some quality work clothes for that next, better job opportunity? It doesn't come easy to be able to look over what you earn and put your money in places that'll help you in the long-term, but it's crucial if you want to break into that abundant life.

Even though we're all given one common finish line to measure success, not all of us have the same starting point. Sometimes, this stems from institutionalized racism, classism, sexism, or ableism, and it can be frustrating; it can even feel like there's no way to break out. While there's someone out there whose life has been set for them out the cradle, their parents hanging with the people who will give them their first job, send them to college, and jettison them to a comfortable life, there are many more of us who have had to fight tooth and nail for the things we have. Those of us that worked our way from the bottom used social capital, our drive, and a lot of hard work.

It's okay to feel frustrated about inequality, but it's important to work through your feelings to make it to the other side. And while it's a bummer to admit, nobody is going to swoop in and hand us all the things others got from birth. Instead, it's on us to carve those opportunities for ourselves. Ask yourself: *what am I surrounding yourself with? What could I be doing with all those hours instead?*

Look back at your first two lists in this chapter; this time, you'll make a third one. List the top ten things that fill up your life. This can be how you spend your free time (drinking, on Xbox) as well as the physical objects in your life (beer, a pipe, a book). And again—be honest. In the second column, write down why you surround yourself with these things. Finally, mark whether these things help you be alive and free or if they're marching you straight off a canyon.

Make the Move

10 key things in your life	Why are these so important?	Reppin'	Misreppin'

How do the things in your life stack up against the people and the places?

Change starts with you. And out of all three facets in this chapter, you're in luck. Shifting the things that occupy your day is the easiest of all three. All it takes is some strength and drive. What can you change today?

I know it's hard trying to make it on your own too, surviving at the same time going to school. And trying to pay tuition by washing dishes, it's all a part of being self-sufficient.

- Fashawn

UNIVERSAL SUCCESS HABIT SIX:

Successful Young Adults Consistently Work to Build Their FEO and They Don't Let Anyone or Anything Mess with It.

Elia's phone alarm went off and she groaned. Five a.m. Again. Hoisting herself from bed, the sun still not up, she moved through her morning routine of brushing her teeth with her eyes half-closed, eating cereal in the quiet house, and heading out by six—right around the time her mom and brothers woke up.

Six months earlier, when Elia had graduated from high school, she'd felt on top of the world. She was a graduate. She was sure she could accomplish anything with a diploma by her side. She already envisioned herself heading home with paychecks to a cute little place she lived at with her best friends. They'd decorate the place with cute pictures, go to the movies or out to lunch when they wanted, and have a happy life. She was set. After all, her sister Kat had a high school diploma, and look at her. Jobs would be lining up to hire Elia; weren't there always opportunities around town? Hiring signs hung outside of coffee shops and restaurants? She'd be fine.

Or so she thought. Now, graduation was a distant memory, and she was desperate to stop burdening her mom financially. Bagging groceries down the street didn't quite pay what she'd been daydreaming about. Minimum wage, it turned out, had been all she could wrangle. With that money, she couldn't even afford to buy a car, and yanking herself from bed to walk the cold mile to work, only to have another morning of busy people micromanaging her bagging skills, was pure torture.

That morning, as Elia's steps echoed off the frozen pavement, she passed people getting coffee in a drive-thru and snorted. How'd they make enough to afford a latte each morning? Here she was, not even having to pay rent, and she scraped by on the acrid breakroom coffee, sitting on metal chairs, her only view the cement floors and walk-in freezer doors.

At the end of another eight hours ringing people up, Elia picked things up for dinner. Tonight it was lasagna. Cooking cleared her head and lightened the guilt of her mom paying her rent. As much as her mom loved her, Elia's two brothers were still in elementary school, and her mom only made $12 an hour. Making—and paying for—dinner helped.

Tonight, Kat was coming over, abandoning the sanctuary of her cute apartment and its bright colors to grace them with her presence. She struggled to stifle her resentment as she unlocked the front door. It was easier once she started cooking. Kat was five years older, anyway. She'd get to that point herself, right? Elia turned up the radio and sang along, pushing her frustration aside. By the time her little brothers walked through the door off the bus, her smile for them was genuine. They wandered into the kitchen, eager to sample the ricotta blend and sautéed zucchini she'd whipped up. They helped her layer the ingredients in the pan before she popped it in the oven in time for her mom to get home to a cooked dinner.

Elia was just setting the table when Kat walked through the door. Her coat looked new. Elia swallowed her feeling of despair. "You look nice."

"Thanks! I got it on sale."

Elia mumbled about needing to get the lasagna out of the oven, leaving Kat in the living room with their brothers.

At dinner, Kat and their mom chatted happily, oblivious to Elia's frustration. Elia sighed, stabbing at her lasagna. They just didn't realize how hard it was, how frustrated she felt that she was still living at home—no car, no prospects. She was trying as hard as she could. The dinner passed with Elia grunting monosyllabic answers and her brothers babbling away. Kids, Elia thought, had it easy.

When her family finished scraping the last of the cheese from their plates and onto their forks, Elia got up. "I'll clean."

Kat rose too. "Let me help."

Before Elia could tell her not to, she had already grabbed a handful of dishes and walked to the kitchen. "I wash, you load." She smiled at Elia. They washed for a few minutes in silence before Kat glanced over at her. "So, you got something on your mind? You've been real quiet, El."

Elia's throat got tight. "It's just. I'm trying so hard. I graduated high school, didn't I? Why can't I find a job that gets me out of here? I'm tired of mom needing to live in a bigger apartment to fit me, throwing some money at her but having it never be enough. I'm tired of being a burden. I just...I wanna start my life but making minimum wage won't even get me enough to buy a clunker! How come you did it so easily, huh?"

Kat laughed. "Elia! I feel you. Don't you remember how I was stuck here almost a year after I graduated?"

Elia blushed. "I forgot."

"I didn't. It was awful. And then one day, I met someone, a lady, while I was working at that coffee shop—remember? She came in almost every day, working on her computer. I finally asked what she did there so often, and she told me about coding. She told me to look into it on YouTube and on a bunch of other websites with free information on learning how, and I did. I really took to it. It wasn't long after that I got my foot in the door doing some basic stuff for people. After that, I learned on the job. I only made a little money at first, but I turned it around in a year and a half. High school diplomas aren't enough. You gotta find something you like." Kat nudged Elia with her elbow. "You're a pretty good cook, maybe that's something you can do."

That night, Elia couldn't sleep. She pulled up her phone and started scrolling through YouTube videos, looking at basic cooking techniques. On her next shift at work, she bought ingredients to try a new technique. Once she started putting her mind to cooking, the month flew by. Elia was amazed at how much she'd learned in only a month; her sister had been right. Armed with an arsenal of free knowledge, she went job hunting— this time in kitchens. When she lucked out and snagged an interview, Elia rattled off all the skills she'd mastered on her own and the boss was impressed. After the interview, he called her boss at the grocery store and was told she was a dependable hard worker and decided to take a chance on her. He wasn't disappointed.

Within months, Elia had earned a raise, and she had saved up for her car. It wasn't long after that she got to move out and pursue her dreams, learning many new skills on the job and becoming a successful chef.

6.1. You're in Control

Elia got out of her situation by realizing something big: being successful means taking control of your own money and positioning yourself for success. She learned that a diploma alone won't cut it; sometimes you have to take the plunge and do the work, whatever that made be, to build up your FEO.

Successful young adults don't let anyone mess with their FEO, realizing it's not only about education; it's about their future. If you're reading this and rolling your eyes, thinking there's some loophole to make quick and fast money, step back for a second—swhat have you got to lose by doing this the right way?

Looking ahead matters. Planning and caring for your FEO is what lands you a full-time job, decent income, health insurance, and your own home. It frees you from being dependent on government assistance and funds hobbies and even vacations, but if you drop out of high school, your expected lifetime earnings will be around $1,115,000. While that may sound like a lot, you could be earning much more.

By taking your education more seriously and completing high school (or getting your GED plus some community college credits) you boost those lifetime earnings to around $1,545,000. By simply failing to complete high school, you're denying yourself roughly $430,000. It makes a lot more sense (and cents) to be serious about your FEO, doesn't it?

That $430,000 could get you a home, send two kids to college for four years, get you a new car every five years between the ages of twenty and fifty-five, pay all of your social security and income taxes, and still save you $11,900 for retirement. All of that just for getting your high school diploma. Are you curious now about how much you'll lose personally for not completing high school? Use the formula below to calculate exactly what your loss of income would be.

1) 65 (retirement age) – ____ (your current age) = ____ (your remaining working years)

2) $430,000 / _____ (your remaining working years) =

_____

(your loss per year for not taking success seriously)

3) _____ (loss per year) / 12 = _____ (loss per month)

4) _____ (loss per month) / 4 = _____ (loss per week)

5) _____ (loss per week) / 7 = _____ (loss per day)

What could you accomplish with that extra cash on a monthly basis? A daily basis? Gen Z wants to get paid and make it big—we all do, don't we? But most of us aren't going to fall into a record deal or MLB contract. So why are you letting people mess with your money? Why are you letting your opinions on school, or the people in it, keep you from that $430,000?

That $430,000 works out to about $105,000 a year you earn for every year you successfully complete high school. Look, if someone had $105,000 for you all wrapped up and ready to go, what would you do to get your hands on it? What if someone told you all you had to do was get through one year of high school with a B average—would you do it? Could you manage that one task for over a hundred grand? If you're like most young folks, you'd do something much crazier for that much money, but are you acting like it?

Let's break it down a little further. Based on a school calendar year (about 160 to 180 days actively at school), you earn about $600 for each day you just show up. Now, is that day you skipped to smoke or drink with your friends worth $600? Let's do another bit of math and find out how much money you missed last year alone:

$600 x _____ (amount of school days you missed last year) =

_____

If you missed ten days, you may as well have walked away from $6,000. Six thousand dollars! Now if you really don't want anyone messing with your money, why are you letting other folks —whether they're asking you to ditch school or presenting you with temptations— mess with your money like this?

6.2. Kicking the Unemployment Training Program to the Curb

By not taking success seriously, you are committing economic suicide. A small segment of young folks unconsciously prepare for failure, and they're doing a great job at it. These young people have enrolled themselves in the "Unemployment Training Program." Hopefully, one of those people isn't you.

Unemployment training is a state of mind that leads you to failure in the working world. Enrollment is simple: all you have to do is not take your education and skills seriously, and you're all signed up.

One way to tell if you're enrolled in the Unemployment Training Program is by assessing if you ever learn outside of school. Those folks destined to fail are those who rarely take books home, and when they do, they never open them. Those same people study for an exam the period before the test is scheduled and never prepare for assignments or follow up on missed ones. Does this sound like someone you know? Does this sound like you?

Another clear symptom of someone enrolled in the Unemployment Training System is their attitude towards attendance or punctuality. In Unemployment Training, students train themselves so well in barely showing up that they become experts in getting fired from jobs. The masters of skipping classes and making excuses, they carry that attitude to the workplace and then wonder why they're having such a hard time holding down a job.

Look at your peers. Has failing to show up really served them? Have they gotten to break out of the cycle of misery and hustling? Or have the classmates who've shxown up been the ones to go on and get scholarships, opportunities, and references?

Let's look at two students. The first one, Derek, is enrolled in the Unemployment Training System. And he forgot his book report. Again. His English teacher pulled him aside after class to ask about it.

"I don't know where it's at."

"What do you mean you don't know? All book reports were due a

week ago, Derek."

"Get off my back!"

"If you don't bring it in, you won't be able to graduate."

"Why are you trying to dis me?"

Heard this before? Unemployment Training students need to be forced into doing things for class and fail to see the value in these activities. It's so hardwired that they don't even know how to answer the door when opportunity knocks, having taught themselves to be passive players when what they ought to do is become active go-getters to make it in the modern world. They let the *now* interfere with their long-term earnings. You can spot guys like Derek from a mile away because of their excuses for everything: why they missed a class, why they failed, why they don't have the homework. By focusing on excuses, they ignore the value of what they missed.

The real issue isn't that excuse, it's the lack of thought about what comes next. Regardless of how legit the excuse is, missing your education has serious consequences—and no excuse changes that.

Let's look at the second student, named Morella. She missed the book report due date as well. Like Derek, her teacher pulled her aside to ask for it. Morella's answer? Completely different.

"I'm sorry; how can I make it up?"

"If you turn it in by the end of the week, I can give you partial credit."

"Great! Thank you, I'm on it."

She's not making excuses, she's looking to succeed—and that simple attitude shift can make or break your future success.

Students like Derek believe that everything always has to be fun; being caught in the Unemployment Training System, they only show up to classes that are fun and interesting, letting all their other classes and assignments pile up and fall to the wayside.

Do you honestly believe that everything you ever do again will be fun? You're in for a rough ride down the line. By believing this mentality, you're preparing to fail at the millions of non-entertaining tasks that life throws at you. Doing the work that isn't fun opens you up to opportunities you wouldn't have been able to if you'd just turned away anything that hinted of work. Yes, it may be unfair that your teacher is boring. But should that boredom keep you from doing your absolute best? You've got two options:

1. Overcome your boredom and your school's shortcomings by taking responsibility for your actions and education

2. Enroll in the Unemployment Training System

Whichever option you choose, remember that over your lifetime, there's a $430,000 difference between those with a high school diploma and those without. Making the most of a boring class sounds like a fair trade for $430,000. Techniques to make it in school are there for you. You can adopt a positive outlook and get online to find resources to help you. You can visit your library and ask about sources to help students do better—there are dozens of books on the subject—but don't even think of making excuses. If you want to be a success, you have to take the reins in your life and not let anyone or anything else sway you from that goal.

Avoiding the Unemployment Training System is simple: stop subscribing to it. If you've never had someone around to teach you positive study habits, test-taking skills, or classroom strategies, take time to investigate these things yourself. Remember: we've got the internet at our disposal. Just ask Brother Yo-Utu-Be. His government name is YouTube. YouTube will show you how to make it in any field out there. Now that we're reaching the end of the book, you're hopefully starting to see that the Unemployment Training System isn't a long-term solution. The first step is choosing to shift your attitude. All the technical tricks and tips? You can find them out along the way.

To hold yourself accountable and get the ball rolling, try telling your teachers you plan to improve your grades and ask them to join your hub (see 2.7). They'll be more than happy to help you, share resources, and give you a leg up down the road.

That path to success is populated with lifelong learners, those who seek out opportunities for knowledge and growth at every chance they get. Lifelong learners hold the keys to their FEO: persistence, hard work, and consistency. It's your choice who you're going to be. Don't let anyone mess with your FEO—even yourself.

6.3. Breaking Down FEO

FEO isn't just the money in your wallet or bank account. It's your opportunities. Your years right now—between 16 and 24—aren't your wealth-building years. Those come later. Now, you're in your FEO-building years, where you focus on making the connections you need to develop your FEO. Start by looking at these five sides of FEO and thinking about how you can start today:

1. Work experience

Early work experience is key to your future success. And we mean legit work: paid, taxed, regulated. Research from the University of Virginia and Middle Tennessee State University has found that twenty hours of part-time work a week in your senior year may result in annual income that's 2% higher six to nine years after graduation, compared to the income of fellow students who didn't work.[1] Just don't go working more than twenty hours—if you're too caught up in punching a time clock, how could you build those other elements of your FEO?

What it is about a part-time job helps you so much? Even if the job is bagging groceries, that work experience tells any future employer that you can show up on time. It shows that people can trust you with money and customers and that employers can count on you to do your job. Long story short: a part-time job tells employers you have what it takes to get a job done. Having work experience also secures your first reference: your boss. Having a boss who can say that you work hard will go a long way. Moreover, having work experience means that you will be around other working people, exchanging that valuable social capital. And while you're working, you gain important soft skills like communication, conflict resolution, and time management.

Over seventy-five percent of the people in this program have had a job before yet don't have any work experience. Why? Because they got fired or left without notice, burning bridges that could have landed them new, better-paying jobs. Don't make the same mistake.

Make the Move

Name three organizations in your community that can help you secure work experience.		
1.		
2.		
3.		

Name three people in your community that can help you secure work experience.		
1.		
2.		
3.		

Name three internet job boards that can help you secure work experience.		
1.		
2.		
3.		

2. Work-related skills

Skill mastery doesn't take place in a classroom; it takes place on the job. The best way to learn a skill is to go out and do it again and again. To really make it, start by identifying what skills you need to develop in a particular field. The safest bet to is to ask someone established in the industry for advice or guidance. Information gleaned from this group is more relevant than any other source. And if you don't know anyone in the industry, remember the internet. Look for videos or articles by people who are in the industry that can give you advice on how to get started.

If you're looking for the basics to get you that first resume-building job, a good place to start is getting the skills to nail your first interview, like how to tie a tie, how to answer ten commonly asked interview questions, and how to make a mock phone call to inquire about a job opening or to set up an appointment. Before heading to an interview, make sure you know how to answer this question:

Have you ever heard the phrase "going the extra mile?" When have you gone the extra mile in work or school?

_____

_____

Second, be able to talk about yourself for sixty seconds without saying "um," "uh," or "ah." Practice when you're alone, and time yourself. With these two talking points in your back pocket (and knowing how to tie a tie if you wear one), you'll be ahead of 84% of the other participants in the MAKiN iT program. These skills aren't hard to come by; there are tons of free resources to start honing work-relevant skills now. Get online, get searching, and build up that social capital.

Make the Move

Visit five employers and ask them what skills are necessary for an entry to mid-level position in their company. Write them here:

_____

_____

_____

_____

_____

_____

_____

What do you need to do to develop those skills?

_____

_____

_____

_____

_____

3. Connections

As you know from section 2.6, the best way to find a job is by going out there and establishing relationships with key people. That's why Chapter Two is entirely dedicated to making those connections.

Remember: most people get jobs based on people they know. You may have some credibility-building ahead of you, but if you're working through this book, you already have a lot to show for yourself. Your dedication to your improvement will be a sure-fire sign to any adult you meet that you're on the right path.

Make the Move

Who are some gainfully employed people you know?	What is their contact info?

Make a plan to help develop your social capital with a diverse group of adults. Establish a good relationship with your bosses and teachers, and don't forget that social capital defines your FEO—your social capital is built on your credibility and rapport, so show up when you say you will. Follow through. It'll make all the difference. And who knows? Those connections you make could pave the way for you to cash in down the road.

With that list in hand, choose one MAKiN iT activity you've completed and share what you learned from it with each person.

4. Industry-recognized credentials

During the 20th century, the world changed beyond recognition. People moved from working in the fields to working in factories. And now, twenty years deep in the 21st century, we're going through a different kind of revolution: The Technological Revolution. Nowadays, there's more technology in a musical birthday card than there was in any computer before 1945.

Where do you fit in this revolution? Will you take part, or will you be left behind because of limited technical skills? Back in the Industrial Revolution, people didn't sit back and say, "Gee, it looks like the

Industrial Revolution is coming, we'd better get prepared." Many folks were unaware that it was even happening. And if you look around now, you'll see the same thing unfolding nationwide. You're lucky, because now you know, and now you have two choices: get up to speed or get left in the dust.

Make the Move (A):

Visit five employers and ask them what credentials are necessary for an entry to mid-level position at their company. Write your findings here.

_____

_____

_____

_____

Where should you go to secure these credentials? Write ideas here.

_____

_____

_____

_____

Make the Move (B):

Think about the various jobs that computers are creating. List them.

_____

_____

How can you make sure you get skills in these areas?

_____

_____

Keep this list you made in the back of your mind and think about how these skills fit into whatever career you're interested in exploring, but also consider this: it isn't just technology that's evolving. Nowadays, our country's workforce is team-oriented and more diverse than ever before, and our country is only getting more culturally diverse. By 2030, people of color will no longer be the minority. If you're eighteen now, you'll be thirty by then and entering your prime working years. You'll be part of the labor force that's responsible for dealing with the challenges created by both diversity and technology. If you have no clue what's going on now, how will you be ready for it in a decade?

In order to really get the skills you need in this changing landscape, develop skills that the older generations never had to worry about. You have to speak multiple languages (preferably Spanish), embrace diversity in the workplace, and master the use of technology. It's your choice if you'll keep up, but the evolving workforce isn't going to wait for you.

Of course, all of this is made much easier with the fifth facet of FEO.

5. Education

In 5.5, we already talked about the stressful reality of education, but its pitfalls don't make it less valuable. Getting an education goes beyond the grades and diplomas. When you're in school, you're filled in on technological trends. You get access to free resources like resume-writing centers, educational speakers, diverse music or art experiences, and career centers, broadening your point of view and connecting you to folks who may hold the keys to your future.

Education can launch you into the future if you use it wisely. Don't let it go out the window because you have a tough time believing in the benefit of broadening your circle of influence. Think about it this way: affluent young people learn all these things as a mandatory part of growing up. They witness firsthand the power of connections by watching their parents' alumni associations, business networks, and professional associates open doors for them. Not all of us have had these opportunities, and it's okay to feel frustrated by it. But take that energy, that frustration, and transform it into drive to learn these five facets of your FEO and start climbing up that ladder to success.

6.4. Real Talk

Let's look back on that money that a high school graduate makes: $1,545,000. Sounds great—until you do the math. It turns out that $1,545,000 only averages out to about $15 an hour. Now are you working your way through all of this to only earn $15 an hour for the rest of your working life?

You're worth more than $15 an hour. It's just up to you to convince yourself you can. If you've made it this far, you've already taken the first steps—now you have to see them through. It's not only about a job or your education; it's about consistently building the five elements of FEO that will help you enjoy a solid, economically stable future. It's all about the FEO.

Still skeptical? That's understandable. Most of the information about young adults on television and in magazines involves a young person doing something negative. Why would you believe that you can make it when all you're fed is despair and failure?

But the truth is that there are millions of young folks out there succeeding, and there's no reason one of them can't be you, so start building up your FEO now to reap those rewards for the rest of your life. Remember: don't let anyone mess with your money—not even yourself.

Let's take a minute to recap.

Why might a young person (maybe you) let someone mess with their money (FEO)?

_____

_____

Interview a young person you know who never lets others mess with their money (FEO). How do they do it?

_____

_____

What are a few things you can do to make sure nobody ever messes with your money (FEO)?

_____

_____

6.5. Attitude is Everything

Success is work. We know it is. But if you believe you can make it, then it doesn't matter where you're starting from. All that matters is where you see yourself heading.

Consider two high school dropouts: both attended the same school, had the same classes and teachers, and came from similar households and economic conditions. One goes on to become a federal circuit court judge. The other? A career criminal.

The difference is their outlook. The second one saw only despair while the other saw opportunity and hope. How you see the world influences what you do and how you act. If you believe there are opportunities available for you in society, you're probably more willing to participate in FEO-building activities than if you think otherwise. The benefit of a positive outlook is non-negotiable. It's the difference between success and failure.

How do you create a positive outlook, especially in a society where power, privilege and injustice seem to rule the day? Remember— those things *don't* rule the day. There are way more compassionate, caring, and committed people out there to help you then there are those trying to hurt you. Start off by realizing that most of your assumptions— especially negative ones—are untested and unexamined. You may feel that school isn't concerned with your education or that society has no real interest in your success, but how can you be so sure that that's the way things really are? Step one in dealing with these assumptions is acknowledging them. The next step is putting them to the test. Ask yourself, "Does this assumption promote my life, freedom, and future economic opportunity?" "What do I need to do to move up the scale?" "Who can I ask to help?"

It is hard to trust others. The immediate results mindset and too many misrepresenters have made certain of that. There is a lot of love out there for you—you just have to find it. This book is one way we are reaching out because in the end, any represter, especially the one writing this book, knows that the healing happens when love touches the pain.

This work isn't always easy. Sometimes our assumptions are so entrenched that they overshadow all other experiences. When you're trapped in an environment filled with violence, death, and surviving by any means necessary, you may shut out positive messages from teachers or concerned adults because what you see overpowers what they're saying. People caught up in the immediate-results mindset resist outlooks that differ from their own. They defend their position even though it may lead to death, loss of freedom, or a lack of FEO. In this stubbornness, they fail to give themselves a chance to make it.

How do you get past the immediate-results mindset? While it may not always be a cake walk, the answer itself is simple: Live by the MAKiN iT Universal Habits Success. They won't lead you astray. Just remember: there are no right answers. All you have to do is make decisions that promote your life, freedom, and FEO.

6.6. Plan Accordingly

A split-second decision can change the rest of your life for better or for worse. Don't let those moments catch you off guard. Build possibilities, opportunities, and connections now so that you're prepared down the line.

If you sit around and wait for the world to get handed over on a silver platter, you're going to be waiting a very long time. Life isn't easy, and at the end of the day, the way you respond to hurdles will determine your success. Attitude is everything. Life can seem like a series of sacrifices, compromises, and hard work, but it all pays off, often sooner than you think, when you've got an education, good skills, work experience, and a positive support network in your corner. It's up to you to make it happen.

Who are the people and what are the places and things in my community that connect people to opportunities, stability, and educational achievement?

_____

_____

_____

_____

_____

_____

You have what it takes to be a success. And now, you've completed a number of exercises geared toward giving you a clearer understanding of where you are and where' you're going. Now it's time to lay that plan out. Planning is critical. It gives you time to examine what you really want to do and allows you to check your progress on a regular basis. If you get off track, don't sweat it. Just adjust and keep going. Life will happen; sometimes minor deviations are inevitable. The key is not to stray too far from the plan.

Do you know most common difficulty people face when sticking to their plan? Personal weakness. For example, it won't make a difference how well you plan your meals and how much you spend on a personal trainer if you end up stopping at McDonalds instead of the gym, right?

Refer to your answers in previous exercises to help you complete your plan. Kick off with your purpose statement, review the skills and behaviors you want to develop, read over the goals you would like to achieve, and recommit to the things you said you wanted to do—and hold yourself to it. If you still haven't interviewed three or four successful young people, write that down in your plan. Watching what you want to do is important if you hope to reach where you want to be.

Below is a sample outline for keeping yourself on track. Think of it as a place to start. Each week, you should have at least four goals to work on. If you're feeling lost, a great place springboard is the following four goals:

1. Consistently promote your life and freedom – and stay away from the things that don't.
2. Build future economic opportunity.
3. Build social capital.
4. Build positive emotions and manage negative ones.

Use this outline for each goal. Write out the goal ("Build positive emotions and manage negative ones"). Below, add any challenges or barriers ("I don't have access to a good mental health professional"). Next, brainstorm some resources or help ("school or programs, coworkers, teachers, support groups"). Finally, give yourself one concrete action or strategy to work toward that this week ("join a meditation meet-up group in my local area").

Remember, if one of these goals doesn't help you realize your purpose, think it over! We have included a master copy of this form at the end of the book; make as many copies as needed, or just rewrite it onto a blank piece of paper if no copier is available.

"MAKIN IT" PLAN FOR SUCCESS:

Goal(s)/Objective(s): _____

Challenges/Barriers: _____

Resources/Help: _____

Task/Action/Strategy: _____

Time Frame: Start Date _____ Finish Date _____

6.7. Getting Paid Creatively

When most young people think of work, their minds jump ahead to getting paid. What they don't realize is that there are many ways of getting paid; it's not always about the money. It's just as worthwhile to invest in learning new skills and connections that will lead you to your FEO.

Sometimes a non-paid position can have more returns than a paid one. The skills you learn, the connections you develop, and the career opportunities you're exposed to can impact your future far more than if you took a job making $8.25 an hour ringing up groceries.

Due to how competitive breaking into a good-paying position can be, many college graduates have taken to volunteering their time to gain quality experience, skills, and contacts. Once they have those resources under their belt, they can use them to get the (paid) job they want. And if you're serious about success, you may want to follow a similar game plan.

In a non-paid work experience, you get a taste of the real-world workforce, learn new skills, and make critical contacts. In many cases, non-paid work experiences evolve into full-time, paid employment after only a few months.

There are a number of ways to get quality work experience, and the best way to maximize its value is by focusing on developing those skills that will help you in your next job. To get your head around these types of experiences, we have a list of the different types of work experiences focus on your learning, development, and growth.

Apprenticeships

These are relationships between an employer and employee during which the worker or apprentice learns an occupation through a structured program. Apprenticeships are often sponsored jointly by employers and labor unions or operated by employers and employee associations.

Cooperative Education

This is a structured method of instruction where students alternate or coordinate their high school or higher education studies with a job in a field related to their goals. In cooperative education programs, students and participating businesses develop written training and evaluation plans to guide learning. Students typically receive course credit for both their classroom and work experiences. Credit hours and intensity of placements often vary with each course of study.

Internships

At an internship, students, young people, or recent graduates work for an employer for a specified period (usually a semester) to learn about an industry or occupation. Often, internships can qualify for college credit.

Job Shadowing

Typically a part of career-exploration activities in late middle school or early high school, job shadowing is when a student follows an employee at a firm for a day (or a few days) to learn about a particular occupation or industry. Job shadowing helps students explore a range of career objectives and select a career track for the latter part of high school, or to guide their post-secondary choices.

On-the-Job Training

This entails hands-on training in specific occupational skills that students receive as part of their workplace experiences.

Service Learning

This is an instructional method that blends community service with a structured, school-based opportunity for reflection on that service, emphasizing the relationship between service experiences and academic learning. Although most of these kinds of activities vary by educational purpose, most programs balance students' needs to learn with the recipients' needs for service. Students benefit by gaining skills and knowledge, realizing personal satisfaction, and learning civic responsibility. In return, the community benefits as well by having a local need addressed.

Sometimes these work experiences offer some type of financial reimbursement, either in the form of a wage or a stipend. Additionally, they are almost all offered through schools or educational programs. It's up to you to find out if your program or school offers any of these options. Work is as much about learning as it is about earning.

What work experience opportunities are available in your school, program, or community?

1. _____

2. _____

3. _____

Which of these work experience opportunities would you like to take part in? Why?

1. _____

2. _____

What do you need to do to take advantage of these work experience opportunities?

6.8.   Hustles and Gigs – the Safe Way

If you are trying to make that cash because you got to put food on the table or your baby girl needs to eat, we hear you. We do. Just remember—do it in a way that pushes the six. Growing up in an environment riddled with poverty, joblessness, and drug use is a playground for the immediate-results mindset. You and the people around you start to justify drug-dealing and other nefarious ways of earning money as the only way to make a living. But it's not—it's not even truly living. Illegal money is the devil's money—remember that painting from chapter one? Chasing that illegal fast money is a quick track to losing. But most of the time, you are hustling for sneaker money, not making the loot many people think. A 2003 report by the Sentencing Project found that your average mid-level dealer was making only a little above minimum wage—and most had to hold down a regular job too, while the low-level street dealer was essentially broke.[2] At least with a job, you have some legal recourse to take if you fall victim to wage theft, but in the street game, you're SOL.

So why do so many people get caught up in it? It's addiction—and not just to the drugs sold. Hustling itself is addictive—the quick money, the girls, the guns. The block is hot, and before you know it, you're constantly checking over your shoulders, not knowing who to trust. That edge is a straight up dopamine rush to your dome piece. The more you get, the more you can't stop until it's part of your identity. If you define yourself as drug hustler, then you work hard at being a drug hustler. It's destruction. Call it like it is. And that never-ending loop is only stopped by tragedy or time: it's the start of your demise and a whole lot of problems for you and the baby girl you're trying to give a good life.

Are drug hustlers entrepreneurs? Maybe—if you can get rid of that hustling addiction. To be a true entrepreneur, you have to put up with not taking a salary for up to three years, doing the same boring stuff day in and day out, and being comfortable with selling somebody something that you probably need to convince them they want. It's easy to sell dope to a dope fiend, but have you tried selling a used car? You'll think you've lost it. And entrepreneurship isn't just selling: it's learning and mastering the principles of running a business. You don't need drugs to teach you about supply and demand, pricing, marketing, and accounting. You can learn those things through running a sno-cone stand, a greeting card business, or a coffee shop. If you're looking to be your own boss, get creative. There are many other ways to do it without putting your life, freedom, and FEO at risk.

To become your own boss and run a business, you'll need some start-up capital, and a great place to start earning paper fast is through side hustles. Side hustles are legal activities you can do to earn money in addition to your job, and roughly 49 million Americans are already in on the game.[3] Side hustles come in all forms. Some popular ones are dog walking, food delivery, charging electric scooters, handing out flyers for an event, driving services, modeling at art studios, or odd jobs through apps like Takl. Why do side hustles matter? For many Americans, they're the difference between living paycheck to paycheck and having a little bit saved up. They can help you get grocery money in a pinch. More people in the U.S. are making ends meet exclusively through juggling side hustles.

One of the best sites and blogs on side hustles is *www.sidehustle-nation.com.* There are tons of ideas on how to start and build a side hustle. Through these side hustles, you can gain all of the essential FEO skills you need to be successful:

1. Connections
The cornerstone of side hustles is making connections with other people. Once that first connection you make walking dogs or watering plants sees you're reliable, it won't be long until they're referring you to friends and colleagues looking for the same services.

2. Work Experience
Struggling to get people to hire you in the first place because of all that blank space on your resume? A side hustle is a legitimate way to show future employers you have a strong work ethic and know how to hold yourself accountable on the job.

3. Skills
Side hustles are a wonderful way to lock in the soft skills employers

look for (like time management and time management) as well as hard skills (like computer systems, navigating different apps, and customer service).

4. Degrees
When you're working a side hustle, the biggest perk is its flexibility. When you find yourself in a degree program, having a job that can meld to your class schedule is a huge bonus: you can pay the bills and take the classes you want and need, no problem.

5. Credentials
This links back to connections and experience. As you grow in your side hustle, you'll have free time to investigate your interests and passions and seek out which credentials will help you grow your hustle. If you start writing product reviews for five dollars a pop and learn you love writing, you can figure out which credentials you need under your belt to start writing your own articles and upping your hourly rate.

What kinds of side hustles interest you?

Make the Move

What side hustles would you do?	Who is one person you know who does this?	What do they recommend you do to get started?

Once these side hustles start bringing in legitimate cash, don't go spending it all at once. To make the good money you have to hold off on spending it—and building your skills in financial management is key. There are a lot of free apps and websites to help you budget (like Mint). By learning how to work a budget and save for the future, you'll be able to grow your hustles and fine-tune your successful future.

One thing that makes your side hustle more prosperous? A healthy relationship. It's uncommon knowledge, but a solid relationship is one of your greatest assets on the success journey. According to recent research, about 43% of married couples consider themselves financially stable, while only 29% of single adults feel the same.[4] This doesn't mean you just snag any partner and assume you're home free. The reason a solid couple is more financially abundant is because there's someone in your life holding you accountable. Remember, a good relationship is a partnership: two people on equal footing, keeping pace with each other. When your significant other feels like your number one teammate, you're doing it right. Chances are that if your partner is a true representer, they'll be helping you in that side hustle every step of the way. Don't let love or infatuation lead you away from the six—you have too much going for you for anything less.

It's your move – what'll you do?

It's never too late to get a handle on your success. You've taken a crucial first step by completing MAKiN iT. However, there's much more to making it than reading a book. You have to live every day of your life with success as your goal. Successful young people take responsibility for staying alive and free, and for developing their FEO to become a self-fulfilled person and productive community member. Remember, you can't decide to only try and make it on Mondays, Thursdays, and Sundays. You've got to strive to make it each waking moment of your life. Sound like a lot? Keep in mind the costs you'll pay down the line if you don't, and you'll find it a whole lot easier to put yourself in the MAKiN iT mindset. Now head on back to chapter one and work your way through this book to the end. Don't leave a single line blank. Don't take any shortcuts. You can do it. You've got nothing to lose—and everything to gain.

Alive and Free,

Endnotes
Chapter One

1. Carneval, Anthony P.; Hanson, Andrew R.; and Gulish, Artem. "Failure to Launch: Structural Shift and the New Lost Generation." *Georgetown University Center of Education and the Workforce*. 2013. Accessed December 2018. https://cew.georgetown.edu/cew-reports/failure-to-launch/

2. VeneKlasen, Lisa and Miller, Valerie. *A New Weave of Power, People & Politics: The Action Guide for Advocacy and Citizen Participation*. Oklahoma City: World Neighbors, 2002.

3. VeneKlasen, Lisa and Miller, Valerie. *A New Weave of Power, People & Politics: The Action Guide for Advocacy and Citizen Participation*. Oklahoma City: World Neighbors, 2002.

4. Willis, Naria. "5 Types of Privilege You Probably Have No Idea You're Benefitting From." *Elite Daily*. 19 May 2016. Accessed December 2018. https://www.elitedaily.com/life/privilege-benefiting-from-no-idea/1496370

5. Ray, Kelsey. "Criminalizing Homelessness Comes at a Staggering Cost." *Colorado Independent*. 18 February 2016. Accessed December 2018. https://www.coloradoindependent.com/2016/02/18/criminalizing-homelessness-comes-at-staggering-cost/

6. Clear, James. "Evolution of Anxiety." *James Clear.* 2018. Accessed December 2018. https://jamesclear.com/evolution-of-anxiety

7. Bal, Michelle and van den Bos, Kees. "Blaming for a Better Future: Future Orientation and Associated Intolerance of Personal Uncertainty Lead to Harsher Reactions Toward Innocent Victims." *Personality and Social Psychology Bulletin Volume 38, Issue 7*. 2012. Accessed December 2018. https://doi.org/10.1177/0146167212442970

8. Watts, Tyler W.; Duncan, Greg J.; and Quan, Haonan. "Revisiting the Marshmallow Test: A Conceptual Replication Investigating Links Between Early Delay of Gratification and Later Outcomes." *Psychological Science, Volume 29, Issue 7*. 25 May 2018. Accessed December 2018. https://doi.org/10.1177/0956797618761661.

9. Maslow, A. H. A theory of human motivation. *Psychological Review, Volume 50,* Issue 4. Pages 370-396. 1943. Accessed December 2018. http://dx.doi.org/10.1037/h0054346

10. "How Can Mindsets Be Changed?" *Mindset Works*. 2017. Accessed December 2018. https://www.mindsetworks.com/science/Changing-Mindsets

11. Adler, Lou. "New Survey Reveals 85% of All Jobs are Filled Via Networking." *LinkedIn*. 28 February 2016. Accessed December 2018. https://www.linkedin.com/pulse/new-survey-reveals-85-all-jobs-filled-via-networking-lou-adler/

12. Wolpert, Stewart. "UCLA Neuroscientist's Book Explains Why Social Connection is as Important as Food and Shelter." *UCLA Newsroom.* 10 October 2013. Accessed December 2018. http://newsroom.ucla.edu/releases/we-are-hard-wired-to-be-social-248746.

13. Baumeister, Roy F. and Leary, Mark R. "The Need to Belong: The Need for Interpersonal Attachments as a Fundamental Human Motivation." *Psychological Bulletin, Volume 117, Number 3.* Pages 497-529. 1995. Accessed December 2018. https://pdfs.semanticscholar.org/3dcc/3d262c08f8f4eb8f766ad72f06d580869309.pdf

14. "Prochaska and DiClemente's Stages of Change Model." *UCLA Center for Human Nutrition.* Accessed December 2018. http://www.cellinteractive.com/ucla/physcian_ed/stages_change.html

15. LaMorte, Wayne W. "The Transtheoretical Model (Stages of Change)." *Boston University School of Public Health.* 28 August 2018. Accessed December 2018. http://sphweb.bumc.bu.edu/otlt/MPH-Modules/SB/BehavioralChangeTheories/BehavioralChangeTheories6.html

16. LaMorte, Wayne W. "The Transtheoretical Model (Stages of Change)." *Boston University School of Public Health.* 28 August 2018. Accessed December 2018. http://sphweb.bumc.bu.edu/otlt/MPH-Modules/SB/BehavioralChangeTheories/BehavioralChangeTheories6.html

Chapter Two

1. MacDougall, Lauren. "The Effect of Youth Incarceration on Siblings and the Family." *Shared Justice.* 25 May 2017. Accessed December 2018. http://www.sharedjustice.org/domestic-justice/2017/5/25/the-effect-of-youth-incarceration-on-siblings-and-the-family

2. *A Shared Sentence: The Devastating Toll of Parental Education on Kids, Families, and Communities.* Baltimore, MD: the Anne E. Casey Foundation, 2016.

3. DeVuono-Powell, Saneta; Schweidler, Chris; Walters, Alicia; and Zohrabi, Azadeh. *Who Pays? The True Cost of Incarceration on Families.* Oakland, CA: Ella Baker Center, Forward Together, Research Action Design, 2015.

4. Bergland, Christopher. "3 Specific Ways That Helping Others Benefits Your Brain." *Psychology Today.* 21 February 2016. Accessed December 2018. https://www.psychologytoday.com/us/blog/the-athletes-way/201602/3-specific-ways-helping-others-benefits-your-brain

5. Inagaki, Tristen K.; Bryne Haltom, Kate E.; Suzuki, Shosuke; Jevtic, Ivana; Hornstein, Erica; Bower, Julienne E.; and Eisenberger, Naomi I. "The Neurobiology of Giving Versus Receiving Support: the Role of Stress-Related and Social Reward-Related Neural Activity." *Psychosomatic Medicine, Volume 78, Issue 4.* Pages 443-453. May 2016.

Accessed December 2018. https://journals.lww.com/psychosomaticmed-
icine/Citation/2016/05000/The_Neurobiology_of_Giving_Versus_Receiv-
ing.7.aspx

6. "Understanding Dysfunctional Relationship Patterns in your Family."
Brown Counseling and Psychological Services. 2019. Accessed January
2019. https://www.brown.edu/campus-life/support/counseling-and-psy-
chological-services/index.php?q=dysfunctional-family-relationships

7. "QuickStats: Average Life Expectancy at Birth, by Race and Sex ---
United States, 2000, 2006, and 2007*." *Morbidity and Mortality Weekly.*
30 October 2009. Accessed January 2019. https://www.cdc.gov/mmwr/
preview/mmwrhtml/mm5842a7.htm

8. *Social Capital and the Well-Being of Youth.* Ithaca, NY: Cornell University,
Family Life Development Center, April 2003.

9. Chen, Angela. "A Social Psychologist Explains Why We Should Ask for
Help More Often." *The Verge.* 22 June 2018. Accessed January 2019.
https://www.theverge.com/2018/6/2/17475134/heidi-grant-reinforce-
ments-help-social-psychology

10. Leana, Carrie R. "The Missing Link in School Reform." *Stanford Social
Innovation Review.* 2011. Accessed January 2019. https://ssir.org/arti-
cles/entry/the_missing_link_in_school_reform

11. Corcoran, Betsy. "Education's Latest Secret Trend: Networking." *Edsurge.*
14 August 2018. Accessed January 2019. http://www.edsurge.com/amp/
news/2018-08-14-education-s-latest-secret-trend-networking

12. Morrow, Monika. "Networking, Not Internet Cruising, Still Lands Most
Jobs for Those in Career Transition." *Right Management Manpower-
Group.* 08 May 2013. Accessed January 2019. http://www.right.com/
wps/wcm/connect/right-us-en/home/thoughtwire/categories/talent-work/
networking-not-internet-cruising-still-lands-most-jobs-for-those-in-career-
transition.

13. Belli, Gina. "How Many Jobs are Found Through Networking, Really?"
PayScale. 6 April 2017. Accessed January 2019. https://www.payscale.
com/career-news/2017/04/many-jobs-found-networking

14. McCormick, Tyler H.; Salganik, Matthew J.; and Zheng, Tian. "How Many
People Do You Know? Efficiently Estimating Social Network Size."
Journal of the American Statistical Association. March 2010. https://www.
princeton.edu/~mjs3/mccormick_salganik_zheng10.pdf

15. Makovsky, Ken. "Dunbar's Number: A Key to Networking." *Forbes.*
7 August 2014. Accessed January 2019. https://www.forbes.com/sites/
kenmakovsky/2014/08/07/dunbars-number-and-the-need-for-relation-
ship-management/#55a8fe38397b

16. Herrera, Carla; Grossman, Jean Baldwin; McMaken, Jennifer; Cooney,
Siobhan M.; and Kauh, Tina J. *High School Students as Mentors: Find-*

ings *From the Big Brothers Big Sisters School-Based Mentoring Impact Study*. Philadelphia, PA: Public/Private Ventures, September 2008.

Chapter Three

1. Kirkpatrick, Nicola. "Fight Flight Freeze: How to Recognize it and What to do When it Happens." *Better Help*. 02 January 2019. Accessed January 2019. https://www.betterhelp.com/advice/trauma/fight-flight-freeze-how-to-recognize-it-and-what-to-do-when-it-happens/

2. Nicholson, Nigel. "How Hardwired is Human Behavior?" *Harvard Business Review*, July-August 1998 Issue. Accessed January 2019. https://hbr.org/1998/07/how-hardwired-is-human-behavior.

3. Franks, David D. "Emotion and Perception." *Virginia Commonwealth University Department of Sociology and Anthropology.* 17 March 1999. Accessed January 2019. http://www.people.vcu.edu/~dfranks/emotion-andperception.htm

4. Jones, Stephanie and Kahn, Jennifer. *The Evidence Base for How We Learn: Supporting Students' Social, Emotional, and Academic Development.* Washington, D.C.: The Aspen Institute, 13 September 2017.

5. "What is SEL?" *CASEL*. 2019. Accessed January 2019. https://casel.org/what-is-sel/

6. "Core SEL Competencies." *CASEL*. 2019. Accessed January 2019. https://casel.org/core-competencies/

7. "What are the Statistics of the Abused?" *National Association of Adult Survivors of Child Abuse. 2011.* Accessed January 2019. http://naasca.org/2012-Resources/010812-StaisticsOfChildAbuse.htm

8. "LGBT Youth." *Centers for Disease Control and Prevention.* 21 June 2017. Accessed January 2019. https://www.cdc.gov/lgbthealth/youth.htm

9. Finkelhor, David; Turner, Heather; Shattuck, Anne; and Hamby, Sherry. "Violence, Crime, and Abuse Exposure in a National Sample of Children and Youth." *JAMA Pediatrics.* May 2013. Accessed January 2019. http://www.unh.edu/ccrc/pdf/05-13%20PED%20childhood%20exposure%20to%20violence.pdf

10. "What are the Statistics of the Abused?" *National Association of Adult Survivors of Child Abuse. 2011.* Accessed January 2019. http://naasca.org/2012-Resources/010812-StaisticsOfChildAbuse.htm

11. Finkelhor, David; Turner, Heather; Shattuck, Anne; and Hamby, Sherry. "Violence, Crime, and Abuse Exposure in a National Sample of Children and Youth." *JAMA Pediatrics.* May 2013. Accessed January 2019. http://www.unh.edu/ccrc/pdf/05-13%20PED%20childhood%20exposure%20to%20violence.pdf

12. Finkelhor, David; Turner, Heather; Shattuck, Anne; and Hamby, Sherry. "Violence, Crime, and Abuse Exposure in a National Sample of Children and Youth." *JAMA Pediatrics*. May 2013. Accessed January 2019. http://www.unh.edu/ccrc/pdf/05-13%20PED%20childhood%20exposure%20to%20violence.pdf

13. Finkelhor, David; Turner, Heather; Shattuck, Anne; and Hamby, Sherry. "Violence, Crime, and Abuse Exposure in a National Sample of Children and Youth." *JAMA Pediatrics*. May 2013. Accessed January 2019. http://www.unh.edu/ccrc/pdf/05-13%20PED%20childhood%20exposure%20to%20violence.pdf

14. Finkelhor, David; Turner, Heather; Shattuck, Anne; and Hamby, Sherry. "Violence, Crime, and Abuse Exposure in a National Sample of Children and Youth." *JAMA Pediatrics*. May 2013. Accessed January 2019. http://www.unh.edu/ccrc/pdf/05-13%20PED%20childhood%20exposure%20to%20violence.pdf

15. "Trauma Statistics." *North Dakota Department of Human Services*. Accessed January 2019. https://www.nd.gov/dhs/Info/pubs/docs/mhsa/trauma-statistics.pdf

16. Rowland, Katherine. "Childhood Stress Leaves Genetic Scars." *Science*. 24 April 2012. Accessed January 2019. https://www.sciencemag.org/news/2012/04/childhood-stress-leaves-genetic-scars

17. Hedaya, Robert J. "The Teenager's Brain: Do you Understand your Teenager's Thoughts?" *Psychology* Today. 03 June 2010. Accessed January 2019. https://www.psychologytoday.com/us/blog/health-matters/201006/the-teenagers-brain

18. Chechik, G; Meilijson, I; Ruppin, E. "Synaptic pruning in development: a computational account". *Neural computation, Volume 10, Issue 7*. Pages 1759–1777. 1998.

19. Zimmerman, Angela. "Shift to a Growth Mindset with these 8 Powerful Strategies." *Inc*. 16 October 2016. Accessed January 2019. https://www.inc.com/angelina-zimmerman/the-8-tremendous-ways-for-developing-a-growth-mindset.html

20. Schab, Lisa. *The Self-Esteem Workbook for Teens: Activities to Help You Build Confidence and Achieve Your Goals*. Oakland, CA, Instant Help Book, 1 June 2013.

Chapter Four

1. Danko, William D. and Stanley, Thomas J. *The Millionaire Next Door*. New York, NY: Rosetta Books, 2010.

2. Zakrzewski, Vicki. "Why Don't Students Take Social Emotional Learning Home?" *Greater Good Science Center* at UC Berkeley. 31 March 2016.

Accessed January 2019. https://greatergood.berkeley.edu/article/item/why_dont_students_take_social_emotional_learning_home

3. Baer, Drake. "Malcolm Gladwell Explains What Everyone Gets Wrong About His Famous '10,000 Hour' Rule." *Business Insider*. 2 June 2014. Accessed January 2019. https://www.businessinsider.com/malcolm-gladwell-explains-the-10000-hour-rule-2014-6

4. Lebowitz, Shanna. "A Top Psychologist Says There's Only One Way to Become the Best in your Field – but Not Everyone Agrees." *Business Insider*. 14 February 2018. Accessed January 2019. https://www.businessinsider.com/anders-ericsson-how-to-become-an-expert-at-anything-2016-6

5. Clear, James. "The Beginner's Guide to Deliberate Practice." *James Clear*. 2018. Accessed January 2019. https://jamesclear.com/beginners-guide-deliberate-practice

6. Chechik, G; Meilijson, I; Ruppin, E. "Synaptic pruning in development: a computational account". *Neural computation, Volume 10, Issue 7*. Pages 1759–1777. 1998.

7. Zimmerman, Angela. "Shift to a Growth Mindset with these 8 Powerful Strategies." *Inc*. 16 October 2016. Accessed January 2019. https://www.inc.com/angelina-zimmerman/the-8-tremendous-ways-for-developing-a-growth-mindset.html

8. Briggs, Sara. "25 Ways to Develop a Growth Mindset." *informED*. 10 February 2015. Accessed January 2019. https://www.opencolleges.edu.au/informed/features/develop-a-growth-mindset/

9. Briggs, Sara. "25 Ways to Develop a Growth Mindset." *informED*. 10 February 2015. Accessed January 2019. https://www.opencolleges.edu.au/informed/features/develop-a-growth-mindset/

10. Briggs, Sara. "25 Ways to Develop a Growth Mindset." *informED*. 10 February 2015. Accessed January 2019. https://www.opencolleges.edu.au/informed/features/develop-a-growth-mindset/

11. Scott, S.J. *Habit Stacking: 127 Small Changes to Improve Your Wealth, Health, and Happiness*. Old Town Publishing, 2017.

12. "Habit Stacking: 17 Small Productivity Habits." *Farnam Street*. 2019. Accessed January 2019. https://www.fs.blog/2014/08/habit-stacking/

13. *Solving the Talent Shortage: Build, Buy, Borrow, and Bridge*. Milwaukee, WI: ManpowerGroup, 2018.

14. Mattoon, Melissa. "Understanding the Youth Skills Gap." *Pyxera* Global. 2019. Accessed January 2019. https://www.pyxeraglobal.org/understanding-youth-skills-gap/

15. *Solving the Talent Shortage: Build, Buy, Borrow, and Bridge*. Milwaukee, WI: ManpowerGroup, 2018.

16. Thompson, Cadie. "The Top 10 Skills That Will Be in Demand by All

Employers by 2020." *Business Insider.* 21 January 2016. Accessed January 2019. http://www.businessinsider.com/wef-report-skills-workers-need-2016-1/#10-cognitive-flexibility-will-continue-to-be-an-important-skill-1

17. Thompson, Cadie. "The Top 10 Skills That Will Be in Demand by All Employers by 2020." *Business Insider.* 21 January 2016. Accessed January 2019. http://www.businessinsider.com/wef-report-skills-workers-need-2016-1/#10-cognitive-flexibility-will-continue-to-be-an-important-skill-1

18. Thompson, Cadie. "The Top 10 Skills That Will Be in Demand by All Employers by 2020." *Business Insider.* 21 January 2016. Accessed January 2019. http://www.businessinsider.com/wef-report-skills-workers-need-2016-1/#10-cognitive-flexibility-will-continue-to-be-an-important-skill-1

19. Thompson, Cadie. "The Top 10 Skills That Will Be in Demand by All Employers by 2020." *Business Insider.* 21 January 2016. Accessed January 2019. http://www.businessinsider.com/wef-report-skills-workers-need-2016-1/#10-cognitive-flexibility-will-continue-to-be-an-important-skill-1

20. Thompson, Cadie. "The Top 10 Skills That Will Be in Demand by All Employers by 2020." *Business Insider.* 21 January 2016. Accessed January 2019. http://www.businessinsider.com/wef-report-skills-workers-need-2016-1/#10-cognitive-flexibility-will-continue-to-be-an-important-skill-1

21. Thompson, Cadie. "The Top 10 Skills That Will Be in Demand by All Employers by 2020." *Business Insider.* 21 January 2016. Accessed January 2019. http://www.businessinsider.com/wef-report-skills-workers-need-2016-1/#10-cognitive-flexibility-will-continue-to-be-an-important-skill-1

22. Thompson, Cadie. "The Top 10 Skills That Will Be in Demand by All Employers by 2020." *Business Insider.* 21 January 2016. Accessed January 2019. http://www.businessinsider.com/wef-report-skills-workers-need-2016-1/#10-cognitive-flexibility-will-continue-to-be-an-important-skill-1

23. Thompson, Cadie. "The Top 10 Skills That Will Be in Demand by All Employers by 2020." *Business Insider.* 21 January 2016. Accessed January 2019. http://www.businessinsider.com/wef-report-skills-workers-need-2016-1/#10-cognitive-flexibility-will-continue-to-be-an-important-skill-1

24. Thompson, Cadie. "The Top 10 Skills That Will Be in Demand by All Employers by 2020." *Business Insider.* 21 January 2016. Accessed January 2019. http://www.businessinsider.com/wef-report-skills-workers-need-2016-1/#10-cognitive-flexibility-will-continue-to-be-an-important-skill-1

25. Thompson, Cadie. "The Top 10 Skills That Will Be in Demand by All Employers by 2020." *Business Insider*. 21 January 2016. Accessed January 2019. http://www.businessinsider.com/wef-report-skills-workers-need-2016-1/#10-cognitive-flexibility-will-continue-to-be-an-important-skill-1

26. Hess, Abigail. "The 10 Most In-Demand Skills in 2019, According to LinkedIn." *CNBC*. 6 January 2019. Accessed January 2019. https://www.cnbc.com/2019/01/04/the-30-most-in-demand-skills-in-2019-according-to-linkedin-.html

27. Hess, Abigail. "The 10 Most In-Demand Skills in 2019, According to LinkedIn." *CNBC*. 6 January 2019. Accessed January 2019. https://www.cnbc.com/2019/01/04/the-30-most-in-demand-skills-in-2019-according-to-linkedin-.html

28. Hess, Abigail. "The 10 Most In-Demand Skills in 2019, According to LinkedIn." *CNBC*. 6 January 2019. Accessed January 2019. https://www.cnbc.com/2019/01/04/the-30-most-in-demand-skills-in-2019-according-to-linkedin-.html

Chapter Five

1. Stanton-Salazar, Ricardo D. "A Social Capital Framework for Understanding the Socialization of Racial Minority Children and Youths." *Harvard Educational Review, Volume 67, Issue 1*. 1997.

2. Nike. "Failure." *Youtube*, featuring Michael Jordan. https://www.youtube.com/watch?v=GuXZFQKKF7A

3. Hartl, AC; Laursen, B; and Cillessen, AH. "A Survival Analysis of Adolescent Friendships: the Downside of Dissimilarity." *Psychological Science, Volume 26, Issue 8*. August 2015. Accessed January 2019. https://www.ncbi.nlm.nih.gov/pubmed/26187246

4. Stancil, Will. "School Segregation Is Not a Myth." *The Atlantic*. 14 March 2018. Accessed January 2019. https://www.theatlantic.com/education/archive/2018/03/school-segregation-is-not-a-myth/555614/

5. McPherson, Marian. "Nearly 40% of Minorities Still Live in Segregated Neighborhoods: Study." *Inman*. 29 May 2018. Accessed January 2019. https://www.inman.com/2018/05/29/most-minorities-still-live-in-segregated-neighborhoods-study/

6. Ingraham, Christopher. "Three Quarters of Whites Don't Have Any Non-White Friends." *The Washington Post*. 25 August 2014. Accessed January 2019. https://www.washingtonpost.com/news/wonk/wp/2014/08/25/three-quarters-of-whites-dont-have-any-non-white-friends/?noredirect=on&utm_term=.da3a75207c8e

7. Hamilton, Darrick; Darity Jr., William; Price, Anne E.; Sridharan, Vishnu;

and Tippett, Rebecca. *Umbrellas Don't Make it Rain: Why Studying and Working Hard Isn't Enough for Black Americans.* Durham, NC: National Asset Scorecard and Communities of Color, April 2015.

8. Zessoules, Daniella and Ajilore, Olugbenga. "Wage Gaps and Outcomes in Apprenticeship Programs: the Effects of Gender, Race, and Religion." *Center for American Progress.* 12 December 2018. Accessed January 2019. https://www.americanprogress.org/issues/economy/reports/2018/12/12/462019/wage-gaps-outcomes-apprenticeship-programs/

9. Anderson, Melinda D. "Why the Myth of Meritocracy Hurts Kids of Color." *The Atlantic.* 27 July 2017. Accessed January 2019. https://www.theatlantic.com/education/archive/2017/07/internalizing-the-myth-of-meritocracy/535035/

10. Laurin, Kristin; Kay, Aaron C.; and Shepherd, Steven. "Self-Stereotyping as a Route System Justification." *Social Cognition, Volume 29, System Justification Theory.* Pages 360-375. https://guilfordjournals.com/doi/abs/10.1521/soco.2011.29.3.360

11. Kraemer, Jackie. "Statistic of the Month: Comparing Community College Completion Rates." *National Center on Education and the Economy.* May 2013. Accessed January 2019. http://ncee.org/2013/05/statistic-of-the-month-comparing-community-college-completion-rates/

Chapter Six

1. Baum, Charles L., and Ruhm, Christopher J. "The Changing Benefits of Early Work Experience." *National Bureau of Economic Research.* August 2014. Accessed January 2019. https://www.nber.org/papers/w20413

2. King, Ryan. *The Economics of Drug Selling: a Review of the Research.* Washington, DC: Sentencing Project. April 2003.

3. Berger, Sarah. "Side Hustle Nation: Millennials are Making Major Money with Side Gigs." *Bankrate.* 12 July 2017. Accessed January 2019. https://www.bankrate.com/personal-finance/smart-money/side-hustles-survey/

4. "Hitched or Flying Solo: Who's Better Off Financially?" *TD Ameritrade.* 21 September 2017. Accessed January 2019. https://www.amtd.com/newsroom/press-releases/press-release-details/2017/Hitched-or-Flying-Solo-Whos-Better-Off-Financially/

About the Author

More than 100,000 educators, policy-makers, and young adults unanimously agree that DeJesus' message about the importance of life, freedom and future economic opportunity is an important message that all young people need to hear. Born and raised in the Bronx, NY, DeJesus is a top speaker at over 20 major youth conferences each year. As a former VIBE magazine editor puts it: "DeJesus' message hits home with the weight of a project building falling on your head. And once every brick has touched down, audiences will have a clear idea of what must be done."

Edward DeJesus

Street Credible, Research-Backed and Impact Driven

Thirty years of experience in the trenches in some of the toughest neighborhoods and policy-making environments has prepared DeJesus to reveal the true social, political and cultural dynamics that keep so many youth from educational and workforce success. Through creative and inspirational storytelling mixed with cold hard facts, DeJesus argues that every community has the seeds to set up the structures that make a difference in their youth's future. And, through his message, audiences learn how to make these seeds grow.

Edward DeJesus is the President of DeJesus Solutions. Their mission is "No More Disconnected Youth." In the U.S. today, 4.6 million youth are disconnected from work and school, and millions more are struggling to hold on. DeJesus and his team create policy and programmatic solutions to build future economic opportunities for the most marginalized youth and young adults.

DeJesus is a W.K. Kellogg Foundation National Fellow and holds a Masters of Science in Management and Urban Policy Analysis from the New School for Social Research. He is the author of Making Connections Work and several other titles on youth success. His work has been featured on NPR, in the Washington Post, the Baltimore Sun and the Miami Herald.

He has blended his love for reaching youth with an extraordinary ability to impact policy by conducting research on effective programs that help youth acquire and maintain jobs. DeJesus served as a youth policy expert for the Sar Levitan Center for Youth Policy at John Hopkins University and served on the Task Force on Employment Opportunities for young offenders for the U.S. Office of Juvenile Justice and Delinquency Prevention. He has served as a consultant to the Annie E. Casey Foundation, Charles Stewart Mott Foundation, the U.S. Dept. of Labor, and the National Education Association.

In his spare time, DeJesus competes in Ironman triathlons.

MAKiN' iT

The Six Universal Habits for True Survival and Success

Universal Success Habit One:
Successful Young People Consistently Make Moves to Advance their Lives, Freedom, and Future Economic Opportunity.
Code: Always Push Towards the Six.

Universal Success Habit Two:
Successful Young People Consistently Build and Maintain Relationships with People Who Push the Six.
Code: Follow and Their Today May be Your Tomorrow.

Universal Success Habit Three:
Successful Young People Consistently Build Positive Emotions and Manage Hurtful Ones.
Code: Infinite drama...the only way to stop it is to never start it.

Universal Success Habit Four:
Successful Young Adults Consistently Inventory and Improve Their Skills and Habits.
Code: Two New Skills and One New Habit Every Thirty Days.

Universal Success Habit Five:
Successful Young Adults Consistently Decode Power, Privilege and Injustice in a Way That Helps Them Overcome Any Barriers to Their Success.
Code: Always Decode the Code.

Universal Success Habit Six:
Successful Young Adults Consistently Work to Build Their FEO and They Don't Let Anyone or Anything Mess with It.
Code: Never Let Anyone Mess with Your Money.

BROUGHT TO YOU BY NATIONAL WORKFORCE DEVELOPMENT EXPERT AND AUTHOR

Preparing Youth for Success in Workforce Development Programs and Beyond Shouldn't Be Difficult. Let Edward Help You Communicate the Message That Parents and Schools Have Been Try to Convey for Years.

Curriculum and Mobile App also Available for Schools and Programs.

Includes More than 20 Activities to Reframe Success and Show What it Takes to Achieve it.

SHIPPING INFO:
Name:
Organization:
Address:
City: State: Zip:
Phone:
Email:

BILLING INFO:
Name:
Address:
City:
State:
Zip:

ITEM	QUANTITY	UNIT PRICE		TOTAL
MAKiN' iT		0 - 20: $14.95		
		21 - 100: $12.95		
		100 plus: $10.95		
MAKiN' iT Curriculum		$250.00		
MAKiN' iT SURVIVAL SCALE		$195.85		
MAKING CONNECTIONS WORK		0 - 20: $14.95		
		21 - 100: $12.95		
		100 plus: $10.95		
		Subtotal		

Shipping and Handling: 3% of total order or min of $6.99, whichever is greater.

	TOTAL	

Send order form and payment to:
DeJesus Solutions, 6925 Oakland Mills Rd. #355 Columbia, MD 21045
Or Email form to: office@dejesusspeaks.com

www.edwarddejesus.com

Made in the USA
Middletown, DE
26 September 2020